More Dogs on Main Street

BY TOM CLYDE

COLLECTED FROM THE PARK RECORD

More Dogs on Main Street

Cover design by
David Chaplin

Layout by
Nancy Hull

ISBN 0-9668829-0-3

More Dogs on Main Street

By Tom Clyde

Giardia Springs Mining Co.

Dedication

This book is dedicated to the people of Park City, without whose Range Rovers, mangy dogs, and public officials it would not have been possible. You just couldn't make up a place like this.

Special thanks to the Park Record, who approached me about writing a column back in 1986. The publisher at the time was Jan Wilking. He sold the paper within a month of my first column appearing. I've never been sure if there was a connection. Andy Bernhard has been the publisher since. It's been a joy to work with Teri Orr, Sena Taylor Flanders and Nan Chalat Noaker as editors in that time. They've given me free hand, but have also exercised some key judgments when things went over the edge.

Introduction

Like most of you, I'm not a native of Park City. My family lived in Woodland during the summers and in Salt Lake during the school year. I learned to ski at Alta, but after the Park City Ski Area opened in 1963, I've been skiing here ever since. I moved to Park City in 1982 when I took a job as the City Attorney. It was supposed to be a laid back, easy job that afforded a lot of skiing with good cash flow. After five years, the town doubled in size. I left with bleeding ulcers and shell shock, took a job as an apprentice carpenter and swore never to practice law again. That didn't last, and I ended up practicing law in Park City for another 12 years.

The first election I watched in Park City included a candidate for Mayor named O.D. McGee. His platform was simple, "More Dogs on Main Street." At the time, every bar in town had two dogs on the sidewalk for every patron inside. The "community leaders" were trying to clean up the image of town, which was plenty rough, and the first step was getting rid of the dogs, then the junk cars, and then their owners. That seemed to threaten the existing order of things.

Now, just a few years later, there are more Range Rovers in town than VW buses. We have hanging flower baskets and festive banners on the lamp posts. We have a Ferrari dealership across the street from the laundromat. The junky ski town has been fully gentrified. The only constant is that there are still dogs on Main Street. They just have better pedigrees.

Chapter 1

Twenty Years of Planning and We Still Haven't Got it Right

November 4, 1993

BIRTH OF A YARD CAR

In a recent public opinion poll taken in conjunction with the local election (remember that?) I was surprised to see that 70% of the respondents said they favored putting some cap on the number of building permits issued. I figure that those 70% are all realtors, and like the idea of pushing the prices even higher by creating an artificial shortage of supply. The other 30% surprised me even more. They weren't willing to settle for a cap on new growth. A full 30% of our friends and neighbors thought the Laguna Beach wildfire, that destroyed several hundred houses, was a "growth management tool worth looking into."

When you look at the size of the typical house being built in Park City, I guess it's not too surprising that the owners tend to look at things through the Reagan-era "supply side" theory. They want to regulate things by tightening the supply. If you have a $600,000 mortgage, there is nothing that warms the heart like wildly inflating house prices and a tightened supply.

Some of us, of course, look at things on the demand side, and think we can control growth in Park City by kicking the bottom out of the market just as easily as putting a lid on the supply of new housing. There was a time in the not too distant past when only a few eccentrics, Eskimos, and ski bums were interested in living here. There were some real hardships associated with life in Park City (and I'm not talking about being unable to get reservations at Deer Valley during the Christmas week). Gradually, the City got its act together to a point that snow was regularly plowed from the streets, some of them were actually paved, and water flowed from the faucet every time the tap was opened. There was an investment in the schools and other services.

Then, having created a virtual paradise, and advertised it all around the world, a whole lot of people moved in. Those same people are now saying that paradise will be lost if any more people just like them move to town, and that we have to stop it. To avoid Paradise Lost, we are looking at Paradise Rationed.

We could probably address the problem through reduced services. If it took three days to get plowed out of the back end of Park Meadows on a snowy morning, the appeal of housing there might fade a little. If kids had to travel to school by dog sled because the buses couldn't navigate the streets all winter, parents would either get a snow cat to replace the Range Rover, or maybe be a little less enthusiastic about telling friends to move to Park City where the living is easy.

And don't forget the positive impact of a few rusted out old cars in the front yards. Few things communicate a community's resistance to change better than a collection of rusting pickups in the yard. It has worked pretty well in my neighborhood through the years; there's no reason that it wouldn't work in yours.

So here is a rare opportunity. A special deal just for you. I have an old pickup that is going into forced retirement. It's only 20 years old, but there is enough rust and body cancer for a truck twice that age. It's a wonderfully offensive color. When we bought the truck, it was about the same shade of yellow as highway signs. Through the years, though, it has gradually faded and rusted to a shade that can only be described as reminiscent of a really bad cold.

So, for a short time only, this wonderful old GMC could be delivered to your house, and installed in the yard at a location of your choosing for the modest sum of $500. The truck still runs. In fact, the engine and transmission are in pretty good shape. It might be worth pulling the engine and setting it on the ground next to the truck (at an extra cost). It's just that the body and the frame are not really connected to each other any more. If you were driving along and hit the brakes hard, I have every reason to believe that the frame would stop, but the body would just keep on going when the baling wire broke. "That's why we keep the brakes a little mushy," the mechanic who works on it told me.

But the important thing is that it still runs well enough to drive it right to your site, where it can be artistically placed on your lot. For a short time, as an added bonus at no extra cost, I can deliver the truck to you and smash the windshield (well, finish it off--it's already got a few cracks). In a matter of a few weeks, there will be vermin living in the seat and under the hood, and nightly cat fights underneath it. Who needs Nintendo?

You could pay upwards of $200,000 to protect your view across that vacant lot next door, plus the burdensome property taxes year after year. Or, you can gain effective control over the lot for a modest $500 by buying my old truck and parking it on your front lawn. Ornamental lighting is extra, and may require a building permit.

This being Park City, there are a million regulations about that kind of thing, but, this being the Untied States, you have certain First Amendment Rights that are only partially compromised by living in Park City. If you have the truck installed in the yard by a recognized artist, it becomes a piece of sculpture, not a 20 year old GMC up on blocks. Stick a religious icon on the dash board, and a couple of Ross Perot bumper stickers on back, and even the Park City taste police would be hard pressed to censor your artistic, religious, and political expression.

But other people, less appreciative of the fine arts, would drive by, look at the vacant lot, and decide that it was pretty nice--a great place to build a trophy house--except that they wouldn't want to live next door to some redneck who kept an old truck up on blocks in the front yard.

I can hear the skeptics now, asking if an old truck in the front yard is such a guaranteed regulator on growth, how come I'm willing to part with one for a mere $500. Well, it's a complicated process, and you have to keep things in balance. You see, we need one more subscriber to the Salt Lake Tribune before we can get home delivery in my neighborhood. So I'm willing to part with the old GMC rather than add it to the fleet of yard cars here on the farm. And besides, I still have the '49 Ford dump truck out front to keep a lid on things.

July 13, 1996

HOME ON THE PLASTIC RANGE

[Note: Shortly after the "Cows" ice cream store opened on Main Street, they placed a large plastic Holstein on their front porch as part of the franchise trademark. Like so many other things that don't matter, it became a major public fight, with the owner of the store threatened with jail, she threatening to sue the City back to the stone age, and the community dividing into Pro-cow and Anti-cow factions. Thank heavens we don't have any real problems around here.]

This deal with the cow has really bothered me. You know the cow, that life-sized plastic job that sits outside the ice cream store on Main Street, except when it is in jail on untasteful exposure charges. The owner of the ice cream store seems to be willing to take the Castle to the mat on this one, and I wish them well, but the whole thing is really a sad reflection of what we have become.

The cow sits on a little front porch area of the business. It's not on the City right of way, but in a recessed area of the building facade. That spot, by the way, has a lengthy regulatory history involving fowl as well as ersatz beef. Back a few years, when it was Scrooge's Restaurant, the owner used to set up a huge barbecue there and grill turkey legs during Art Festival.

The artists in front of the business hated it because their art work was almost blackened by the smoke from the barbecue and the grease splatters. People would buy a big sauce covered

13

turkey leg the size of a club and then start wandering the art festival, leaving greasy finger prints up and down the street. In the sort of perverse way that life works, the booths in front of Greasy-Turkey-Legs-R-Us were always selling some sort of textile art work with unique physical properties that made the artwork a magnet for turkey grease.

So in the normal barnyard progression, poultry has been replaced with the Holstein. The cow doesn't smoke, splatter grease, or otherwise mess on the sidewalk. The cow is probably a more desirable citizen than many people, who insist on littering the streets. In fact, I have seen secret plans at the Castle that involve replacing all of the people in Park City with plastic mannequins. That way, the City can control the aesthetics of things completely. They can dress the plastic people in appropriate Ralph Lauren designs, and pose them doing appropriate and tasteful things up and down the street. You can bet that there won't be any of the plastic people posed throwing beer bottles from the deck of the Club to the roof of the Post Office.

These plans are farther along than you might imagine. If you look closely, some of your neighbors are early prototypes of the perfectly tasteful plastic people. They live in look alike houses, wear look alike clothes, and have look alike anxieties that something spontaneous might happen in Park City and destroy the well-ordered predictability of the place.

The City people sort of have a point about the cow. If everybody on Main Street put the life sized plastic mammal of choice out in front, it would look like a bad theme park, instead of looking like a pretty good theme park now. But there probably aren't a half dozen businesses on Main Street that have locations on their own property to put a plastic cow. There probably aren't many businesses who would find any advertising value in having a plastic farm animal out on the porch.

Personally, I like the cow, but then I thought Park City looked better when there were real cows on the entrance to town

14

on a working dairy instead of our museum quality, hermetically sealed open space. But what really bothers me about the cow controversy is the inability to make adjustments. Why is everything so rigid these days?

Years ago, there was a controversy with street vendors. The issue was that catering trucks with loud, obnoxious horns were cruising the neighborhood construction sites to sell lunch to construction workers. Local restaurant owners kind of liked having the construction workers buying lunch on Main Street, and residents weren't sure they needed to hear the catering trucks playing "Dixie" on air horns as they pulled into the construction site next door.

There were also time share salesmen stalking the streets assaulting the unwary with time share sales presentations. So the City Council decided to ban street vending in all its various forms. Except---there was Dennis Feldman, the hot dog guy. Dennis had an authentic New York hot dog vendor cart that he had brought out from New York with him. (How a young man from Brooklyn decided that when he grew up, he wanted to be a hot dog vendor in Park City, Utah is another story.)

Some of the council members had young children at the time, and their kids loved to stop at the side of the road and get a hot dog from the New York Weenie Company every now and then. The operation didn't fit the ordinance, didn't fit the sense of what was tasteful (Vail didn't have a hot dog vendor), didn't fit the master plan and just didn't quite fit anywhere. But it was fun. That used to matter.

The City Council called Dennis in and negotiated a deal that banned street vendors, but grandfathered the previously unlicensed hot dog guy. They asked if five years was long enough to amortize his investment, and he said that if he was still selling hot dogs from a push cart in five years, they should put him out of his misery. With a little give and take, the hot dog guy stayed in business. It added a little spice to Park City. There was something kind of serendipitous about discovering an authentic New York hot dog vendor cart way out West on lower Park Avenue.

The ordinance was probably unconstitutional and discriminatory. It clearly made a special exception for a single business that would not have been made for anybody else. Those were very good hot dogs! But at the time, Park City was the kind of place where that kind of exception could be made without lawyers for ten private businesses and a dozen non-profit special interest groups suing. The community was small enough that people dealt with each other on a personal level. The hot dog vendor exception was not some legislative perk, it was a way to keep Dennis on the streets.

The City's position on the cow may be correct in a strict and even--if heavy--handed application of the regulations. But it sure is fun to watch little kids getting their pictures taken eating a double decker ice cream cone sitting on the back of the cow.

And it was even more fun living in the kind of town where instead of throwing the book at the owner of the cow, the City would try to find a way to accommodate something that people liked but didn't fit within our too-thick regulations.

Ah, the good old days, when plastic cows freely roamed the earth, grazing placidly on Astroturf.

December 22, 1994

CHRISTMAS IN PARK CITY

I was up at the Castle the other day at the Planning Department. A sort of portly old gentleman with a white beard and funny red pants was at the counter trying to get a building permit. As anybody who has tried to get authorization to change a light globe knows, that isn't easily done under the best of circumstances. Most people rely on architects, engineers and lawyers for difficult tasks like choosing a paint color. But this old guy was up there trying to do it himself, and not getting anywhere.

"You realize that your water and sewer fees will be based on the number of bathrooms, don't you?" the planner asked.

"Well, if that's the way it is, I guess that's the way it is."

"You have an awful lot of bathrooms in this house." I took a look at the plans, and the second floor of the house kind of looked like a college dorm.

"I need to make arrangements for the elves. They're small, but they all want a nice bedroom, and a comfortable elf is a happy, efficient elf."

"Elves?" the planner asked. "How many elves are we talking about here?"

17

"Lots and lots of them. It varies from season to season. There are hardly any in January, but by September, I'm hiring, and of course, this time of year, I'm up to full staff."

"And these elves live with you?"

"Oh, yes. I like to have my helpers live right there in the house with me."

"Are you related to all of these elves by blood or marriage?"

"No. They're elves. Little tiny people. I'm not exactly an elf myself." He let out a jolly Ho-ho-ho.

"That appears to put you into the conditional use process for a group home or boarding house. I don't think it is allowed in that zone, and even if the city zoning allowed it, there might be problems with the restrictive covenants in the subdivision. You know how the public reacts to group homes, especially for housing large numbers of juveniles."

"They are elves. Some of them are quite elderly, they are just small so they look like youngsters."

"Well, I'll have to think about how to process this one. It might fit as a boarding house, a bed and breakfast, or a nursing home. But any way you cut it, this is still a conditional use. Are these elves citizens of the United States? Is this program receiving any Federal Funding? If some of the elves are handicapped, we might be able to get around some of the restrictions under some federal programs. What are these elves doing while they are here?"

"They make toys. We turn out a lot of toys in the course of a year."

"Gee, that gets it even more complicated. That kind of light manufacturing is an industrial use and can't go on in a residential area, even as a home occupation. It won't fit because you have too many employees. Well, maybe we could call it come kind of work therapy at the group home for juvenile delinquents. But you really want to be in the Light Industrial

Zone, except that you can't have people living in the factory. Do you have an EPA approved paint spray booth?"

The planner turned the page on the big roll of plans to look at another sheet. There was a long pause and some quick measuring of side yard set backs. "I don't think you can build a garage this big this close to the lot line."

"It's not a garage. That's for the reindeer."

"Reindeer?"

"Yes, the reindeer need a shelter. It's more of a barn than a garage."

"How many reindeer are we talking about here?"

"Eight, but they are small and very well behaved."

"Reindeer don't count as household pets. I think that is an agricultural use. You might get away with one or two horses in that zone, but there is no way we can approve keeping a herd of reindeer. If we did that, we'd have cows and sheep and who-knows-what in every neighborhood in town."

"But I have to keep the reindeer. I use them for transportation. I don't have a driver's license and don't have a car, so I rely on the reindeer to pull my sleigh. They are very clean and quiet."

The planner turned another page, and took a look at the facade of the proposed house. "This will never do. Your design doesn't comply with this week's design guidelines. There are too many lights on the outside. These candy cane pillars on the porch are a violation. You can have peeled logs, but you can't have peeled logs painted to look like candy canes or sculpted like snow men. And this chimney is going to be a problem. Why do you want such a big chimney on a house? I don't think the building department will approved a chimney that size. It doesn't have an Underwriters' Laboratories approved spark arrestor on it. We would prefer to see a metal roof in that location."

"I hate metal roofs," the old gent said. "They are too slick. And spark arrestors are a real nuisance, too. They really slow things down."

The planner put the plans down and said, "There is no way you can build this house in Park City. I suggest that if you want to build a work therapy ranch program for troubled youth that you need to find a site outside the City Limits. I wouldn't want to encourage you in terms of building in the County, either. They have the same kinds of restrictions. I think you better consider looking somewhere in Wyoming."

"Or the North Pole," he muttered. The old man rolled up his plans, and pulled on his red stocking cap. "I'm making a list," he said. "I'm checking it twice to keep track of people who are naughty and folks who are nice. And you, my friend, are getting a lump of coal this year." He picked up his plans and stormed down the hall.

"Suit yourself, but you should know that the air quality board regulations prohibit burning coal," the planner said, "and storage of coal is a mining use that is prohibited in all residential zones."

The next guy got to the window, and the planner shook her head and said, "Boy, we get all kinds this time of year. What can I help you with?"

"I need a permit to build a manger."

July 20, 1996

SMOKING COW PERMIT FUTURES

[Note: About the same time the City decided to crack down on plastic farm animals on Main Street, they abruptly changed Main Street parking requirements and explored regulating fireplaces. The move to regulate fireplaces was apparently motivated more by the fact that Vail and Beaver Creek do it than any real smog problems in Park City. The proposal called for all kinds of transferable fireplace permits that would have required a dozen employees to manage. Ultimately, it ended up as one of the "Let's Make A Deal" aspects of the conditional use process, and you can build more fire places if you do a tasteful job of managing storm drainage on site.]

I had lunch the other day with my old friend Walt the dry wall hanger. It's been a while since I've seen him. His business has been going well lately, and he has been raking it in. A while ago he traded his old truck in on a Range Rover. It's still full of tools and plaster dust, but he goes from job to job in style. The neighbors don't even complain about him parking in front of their houses any more. But Walt still has a tough time following our local affairs. There's just too much plaster dust in those sinus cavities most of the time.

"So did you get your permit yet?" he asked.

I was still puzzled about him ordering the angel hair pasta with pesto sauce instead of his usual chili size with fries, and didn't really understand the question. "What permit."

"Well, you know, that permit from the City you need to get." You need a permit for everything around here, and I was concerned that something had slipped past me. Walt was about

21

to explain the nature of this new permit when his cellular phone rang. He answered the call, and before long was leafing through his Franklin Planner trying to schedule an appointment to bid on another job. After quite an effort, and two other calls, he was able to reschedule his yoga, and move his personal trainer appointment so he could meet the general contractor for a few minutes in early August.

He put the phone down and tried to pick up the thread of our conversation. "See, I heard it on the news. We all have to get a permit from the City. It really doesn't matter what you are doing. You have to get a permit. Even if you aren't doing anything."

I was still confused, but before I could coax a clarification out of Walt, the phone rang again. His hair stylist wanted to change Walt's appointment, and Walt was not sure he could live with himself if he delayed getting his hair styled over the weekend. Walt used to get his hair cut every six months, whether it needed it or not. I think he did it himself with a dry wall knife. Now he was going to a stylist. My how times have changed.

"So what I don't understand about this permit business," he said, "is what I'm supposed to do with the plastic cow."

"Say what?"

"See, I heard on the news that everybody needs to get a permit, and if they get their permit, they are entitled to keep one EPA approved, smoking, plastic cow in the front yard."

"I see."

"But if you want to have more than one plastic cow in the front yard, then you have to find somebody else who already has their plastic cow permit, but doesn't want it, and buy their plastic cow permit. Then you can have two plastic cows in the front yard. Then, on days when somebody decides the air is polluted, you have to bring the cows inside so they can't smoke."

"Smoking isn't good for plastic cows anyway," I said.

"Well, that's the thing. If it's not good for plastic cows to be smoking, why don't we take out all the smoking cows instead of allowing people who like a whole herd of them to buy plastic cows from other people?"

"Well, maybe the second home owners will be less likely to use all those cows, since they aren't here very often."

"And then there is this new fee thing. What about that? If you don't have room to park your plastic cow on your own lot on Main Street, you have to pay a huge fee into the City's fund to buy additional space to park your smoking cow someplace else. And I still don't understand why everybody wants the cows in the first place."

Walt's phone rang again, and his conversation this time was in hushed tones. He was not ordering Sheetrock. From what I could discern from one side of the conversation, Walt and a friend were trying to buy a thousand plastic cows and have them delivered to a house in Deer Valley. If they could get them installed before the new regulations took effect, they would have cornered the market on plastic Holstein futures.

The plan was to have enough pre-permit bovines that whenever anybody in Park City wanted to install more than one plastic cow, they would buy the extras from Walt at whatever price he could get for it. In Walt's strange way of doing business, this was genius. I've heard of people planning to do that with fireplaces. In fact I know of one studio apartment that is packed full of wood burning fireplaces. Nobody can live in the place, it's so full of fireplaces, but the owner plans on making big money selling fireplace permit futures. A whole sub-specialty has developed in the local real estate community dealing with transferable fireplace rights.

Others are trying to figure out how to make a buck with the new parking regulations on Main Street. Those may impose a fee of something like $400,000 on a 2,000 square foot restaurant. That should add something to the price of a cheeseburger. The approach seems to be to make sure that no business smaller than the GAP can afford to locate on Main Street, then adopt other regulations that make sure the GAP can't actually open a store there. So others are trying to figure out how to transfer parking rights between Main Street lots.

But only a genius like Walt would have thought of putting it all together. He was planning to corner the market on transferable smoking plastic cow parking rights.

He finished the call, and put the phone down on the table. "This is huge," he said in a loud whisper. "Huge."

Walt was going to be rich. He was thinking about sail boats and condos in Mexico and taking up golf.

Frankly, I found the whole thing quite disturbing. Walt had always been my conduit to practical reality. Lunch with Walt was a way of getting back in touch with regular guys who did tangible work and went home at the end of the day and played Frisbee with the dog. But not any more. I had to do something.

"So Walt, I think I understand the logic in all of this stuff except for one thing. There's one part I just don't get; one piece that isn't fitting together for me."

"What's that?"

"How are you going to herd the plastic cows across Park Avenue without the ski bridge?"

His face turned ashen, and he almost choked on a marinated artichoke heart. "I didn't even think about that."

He left the restaurant with his cellular phone smoking.

June 27, 1998

GEE, ANOTHER GROWTH
MANAGEMENT FORUM

The City's Department of Dire Millennial Predictions hosted yet another meeting Monday night to talk about growth. Gee, we haven't heard anything on that topic before. The flier advertising the event said they would be talking about the future of Utah, Park City, and the West. "The trends are clearly in motion. Utah's urbanizing Wasatch Front and back will have as many people as San Diego in 2010 and as many as Philadelphia in 2050. Where will all these people live, how will they get around, what open space will be left, and what will Park City and the Snyderville Basin look like? These are serious questions, and the time to ask for answers is right now."

Well, actually the time to answer those questions was about 25 years ago.

Forgive me for sounding a bit jaded, but it seems like we fund one of these meetings to discuss the imminent falling of the sky about every six months. On that schedule, people who are living in houses so new the paint is not yet fully dry can come to meetings and voice their grave concerns about run away growth, and how it must be stopped before somebody builds a house on the vacant lot next door to theirs. We need a growth management plan. Adopt a new code. Invent new regulations. Make it hard to get a building permit. Growth is not easily slowed. It's not like the local political forces have been out there recruiting developers. We've made a pretty solid run at growth management at a local regulatory level here and you can all see how well it's worked. In terms of stemming the tide of population growth, we haven't accomplished anything.

The meeting on Monday went over the same routine, though according to some reports, one of the participants did the unspeakable, and mentioned that the real problem is family planning, not zoning. It really doesn't make a huge difference what the architectural standards are, or how tight the sign code is, or how many acres of park land per person we have. All of those kind of knock the edge off, but if we stick 25,000 people in Snyderville, it won't be a very pleasant place. Most of Utah's growth arrives via the birth canal rather than the moving van. So how do we stop population growth? Well, when a man and woman really love each other . . .

The Chinese have been fairly effective with mandatory sterilization. It would be difficult to get that passed on a ballot initiative in Utah. Then there is injecting contraceptives into the drinking water. Again, that has some political problems; too much like fluoride. And the rich would get around it by drinking bottled water. History's other successful options for knocking back the rate of population growth are war, famine, and disease. I don't think our planners and growth managers are paying adequate attention to these options. If we're serious about holding the population even, or maybe shrinking it a bit, we need to seriously consider war, famine, and disease, and spend less energy yammering about intermodal transportation.

If we're going to thin the population with a war, we need to choose carefully. Wyoming is too well armed. Idaho's militia is pretty well organized. So I lean toward Arizona. If Utah declared war on Arizona, we could probably win. I don't think those old gummers down there would put up much of a fight. But then the casualty rate on our side would be pretty

26

modest. We might gain some territory for re-location of Utah's excess, but we probably wouldn't diminish our own numbers all that much. Utah people could move to Arizona now if they wanted to. I doubt we could beat Colorado in a fair fight, and we certainly don't want to mess with California. If we lost, they would overrun us completely. Also, I think the odds are pretty good that California has the atomic bomb. I'm not sure that war on a neighboring state is the answer.

The problem with famine is that the local economy depends a lot on the restaurant business. It's hard to run an effective famine when there are 50 good restaurants in town. That leaves disease. We've got a stock pile of anthrax out there in Tooele that would thin the herd pretty effectively. But I doubt there is the political backbone among even the most ardent no-growthers to launch an anthrax attack on the Wasatch Front or Los Angeles (well, maybe we could find support for Los Angeles, especially during Film Festival). So the historic means of dealing with population control probably won't work.

There is always the option of making this a less desirable place to live so people move someplace else. That's a sort of pre-emptive strike against the ultimate outcome of the naturally occurring growth. That is, if we keep doing what we are doing, this will eventually not be such a nice place to live. If we can get in front of the quality of life decline, and accelerate certain parts of it, we might be able to get things bad enough, soon enough, to discourage more people from moving in to make it worse.

So you start out by voting down every bond issue. The schools want $93 million for new facilities. If they don't get the money, class sizes will swell, some schools will be on double sessions, and life in the schools won't be so pleasant. "But if people vote no on the bond issue, my kids will have to go to school in classes of 40 kids," you gasp. Yep, that's right. Growth has names and faces. Growth is sitting right there at your dinner table, stuffing down the last pork chop and asking to borrow the car on the weekend to drive to a Phish concert in Denver.

In the end, we keep passing the bond issues, keep the cork in the anthrax bottle, avoid famine, and maintain peaceable relations with other states. The birth rate continues at Bangladesh rates. No wonder we're growing. There were no answers out of the meeting on Monday. The people with all the answers have none, though manage to scratch out a pretty good living giving speeches suggesting that they have answers. Local officials keep saying we have to stop growth, but at the same time, they are so completely addicted to growth related revenues for government operations that a radical slow down would have a devastating impact on their ability to function.

So we hold meetings where we get another dose of the planning stuff. I've come to the conclusion that the serious planners have adopted it as a religion rather than a tool. The basic dogma is that good urban planning could make Calcutta a very nice place. We're searching for right answers to the wrong questions. Nobody will come out in favor of creating an economic depression locally, declaring war on Arizona or anthrax. Instead, we charge full speed ahead on improvements that make the community a magnet for in-migration, marketing the place around the world, and then express great surprise and dismay when people move here.

There is no question that Utah will be the size of San Diego in a few years. Though we are loathe to admit it, we apparently want it that way.

May 31, 1997

INTERMODAL TRANSPORTATION PARADIGM

Last weekend's Memorial Day was kind of a wash out in terms of weather. It only quit raining long enough to snow. I thought about going south, but the weather was supposed to be about the same down there, and a stormy three day weekend up here is a kind of family tradition. The whole extended family was out at the ranch for the weekend. When you put them all together, four generations' worth, it is a crowd bigger than the cast of "Ben Hur."

Pack that many people together for long enough, and all the little peccadilloes start coming out. There are thermostat fiddlers, window openers, 50 different ways of loading the dishwasher, and an iron-clad guarantee that three out of four children under the age of six will be bawling at any given time. A good time was had by all. Various members of the group had other commitments during parts of the weekend, and arrived or left at different times. It was a true American celebration, with everybody bringing their own car, most of them Japanese. There are justifications for that--lots of stuff to carry (babies apparently require a moving van full of equipment just for over night), different schedules, different starting and end points so car pooling wasn't really all that convenient. All the usual excuses.

But by Saturday night, we had a parking problem. The Parking Administrator took some offense at the complaints that there was no parking. After all, there is no shortage of flat, open land on the farm. But nobody wanted to park out at the barnyard and walk back to the house in the snow. There was a shortage of convenient or desirable parking.

So the Parking Administrator decided the solution would be to charge for parking, and came up with a lengthy set of regulations for parking overnight, short term parking, parking for non-standard vehicles (my brother has this 4 door pick-up with dual rear wheels for towing his horse trailer around, and it takes up more dock space than the Queen Elizabeth). Some people thought it was an odd concept to have to pay to park in their own driveway. Others quickly figured out that if they went out and rolled their cars forward a couple of feet every four hours, the chalk mark on the tire would move, and they could avoid a ticket. Some just assumed they could beat the tickets by leaving the jurisdiction.

Another member of the family suggested that if she had to pay to park, she might not be able to come to the cabin as often, or stay as long, because of the high cost of parking. Since about half of the crying babies were hers, the decision was quickly made to increase parking charges substantially, especially for cars with baby seats in them.

Even with these adjustments, we still had a parking problem. Friends started dropping by, and there was no place for them to park. It was so congested that it was hard to get farm machinery down the lane. So we decided to do the only reasonable thing. We hired a consultant.

There are probably people right in the area who could have figured out a solution, but they didn't cost quite enough. So we hired a company out of Boston to study the parking problem in the family driveway. It was into six figures, but the consultant has an excellent graphic design on their report covers. Normally they would have charged us for travel expenses, too, but since they are here working on Park City's $750,000 traffic study anyway, we got a deal.

The consultant set up a series of open houses to find out what we really wanted or expected in terms of traffic and parking around the ranch. They were surprised to learn that people wanted to park close to the house they were staying at. Nobody was pushing for paved roads or clover-leafs. The consultant was surprised to find that not one person said he or she ever wanted to ride a bus.

Based on the public input, the consultant came up with three alternatives to study: (1) Do nothing, which seemed pretty reasonable given the lousy weather; (2) Enhance the current parking situation by encouraging people to park in some sort of organized manner and car pooling when possible; or (3) Intermodal New Age Transportation Paradigm Vector Matrix. Considering the price of the study, it's not too surprising that the consultant favors the Intermodal New Age Transportation Paradigm Vector Matrix alternative. He would look pretty silly charging that much money and suggesting that we do nothing at all.

As best I can figure it out, the Intermodal New Age Transportation Paradigm Vector Matrix is a way of providing transportation alternatives that mostly center on forcing people to ride the bus against their will. None of them will be as comfortable, convenient, or efficient as people driving around in their own cars, but there will be options. "Intermodal" is one of those French diplomatic terms that is difficult to translate. Roughly, it means: "The hired help will be forced to stand in the rain waiting for a bus, and they have to get to the bus stop by kayak because the bus only runs on high volume routes and stops at arbitrary jurisdictional boundaries."

Part of the consultant's plan was the construction of a new "Intermodal Transportation Center, Tofu Cafe, and Wellness Center" that would replace our 100 year old barn. It would have stunning architecture with lots of controversial public art. The Intermodal Center would be the hub where all the various forms of transportation would come together in

31

harmony. For example, an upstream neighbor could float down the river in a kayak to the bridge, then switch to a mountain bike to ride to the Intermodal Center. At the Intermodal Center, there would be a place to park the kayak and bike, and enjoy a latte while waiting for the next "modal" to come. Our traveler could meet a friend and switch to a horse for a side trip up the canyon, or after a considerable wait, catch the cell phone dispatched Smart Van in to town.

Under the plan proposed by the consultant, the person who used the most different forms of transportation on the shortest trip, while carrying the most difficult load, would be rewarded with a new pair of Birkenstock sandals. People who continued to rely on their own cars would be branded as Luddite Monomodals, and ridiculed by everybody standing in rain at the bus stop.

Chapter 2

Festivals, Pageants, and Other Reasons to Leave Town

January 17, 1998

SUNDANCE DOES THE CLASSICS

So here we are at Film Festival again. As usual, tickets are as scarce as good popcorn and convenient parking. In the past, I've had a hard time with Film Festival. I suppose it is partly that I'm a cultural barbarian in many ways. I like a good movie as well as anybody, but I've never quite figured out "art films." They are depressing. A quick flip through the catalog this year yields descriptions of this year's entries like: "It's a dysfunctional landscape of brutish fathers, casual drugs, rejection, and a sense of futility." Boy, I want to see that one. It's apparently a comedy. Another film "reveals the tenuous boundaries between normal and aberrant, perhaps even perverse, needs and desires." Honey, get the kids, let's go to the show!

In truth, most of the films probably aren't half as weird as they try to make them sound, but at Sundance, mainstream is the kiss of death, so everybody tries to make sure their film sounds as weird as possible. Edgy, dark, and a little twisted are the keys to high acceptance. That's not to say that the films aren't artfully made and presented. There are bad weird, disturbing, strange films and there are good weird, disturbing, strange films. Sundance graces us each year with the very best of the weird, the disturbing, and the strange. So hold on to your cell phone, Martha, it's time to go to the movies.

The regular ticket packages were sold out in about July. People were camped out in Swede Alley to buy a place in line to buy whatever tickets were turned back in or for midnight

35

showings. I wouldn't camp out in Swede Alley in January for an audience with the Pope, so I didn't get many tickets. What I did get was a special ticket for a little-publicized part of the Festival called "Sundance Does the Classics." It's a part of the Festival that offers some great movies, I'm sorry, *films*, for the discerning viewer of ordinary and uneducated tastes. Each year, "Sundance Does the Classics" features some of America's favorite movies updated by Sundance artists. All of the old stereotypes that marred the originals are removed. Films are stripped of their cloying sentimentality, expansive scenery, quality camera work, and other undesirable elements. Then these classics are re-told in the politically correct, angst-ridden, drug-addicted style of modern film makers, in grainy black and white with the camera jerking like it was held by a junkie in withdrawal. For example, here are a few classics re-made in the Sundance style:

Gone With the Wind features an obese Scarlet O'Hara who refuses to deal with such silliness as barbecues or corsets, and spends her days campaigning against weightism in a world of chitlins and ham. She is afflicted with numerous eating disorders, and locked in a destructive, co-dependent relationship with the cross-dressing Rhett Butler. Grace Jones turns in a stunning performance as Mammy, the crack dealing slave who stays with Scarlet through thick and thin, and helps make Scarlet and Rhett matching evening gowns from the drapery material. The film was shot entirely on location in Chicago's Cabrini-Green public housing project. The landscape is rich with graffiti and gang violence as the characters deal with the upheaval of the recent welfare reforms. Written and directed by the famous French cinamatist Jacques Merde, who apparently never heard of the Civil War.

Titanic is a big box office success, but hardly fits the Sundance mold. The re-make features a 20-something slacker who spends his time making model ships and getting high sniffing the glue. The protagonist (who we care so little about that he never gets a name in the film) spends most of a year making a beautiful scale model of the Titanic. In a drug induced rage, he then decides to float the boat in the swimming pool of his parents' elegant Bel Aire home, using his sister's pet gerbils as passengers. Instead of an iceberg, the model ship is sunk when he shoots it with a .357, blowing the model ship to smithereens. Those gerbils not killed by the gun shots drown in the swimming pool. A tag line in the credits will assure us that "no actual gerbils were injured in the making of this film." Unfortunately, that is not true of the woman in the house next door who was struck and killed by a stray shot.

The dark, edgy children's classic *Heidi* makes a fresh appearance on the Sundance screen this year. Shot in a soft focus black and white, using a jerky hand held camera, the film follows the tragic life of Heidi, played by Kate Moss, who is a committed vegan. She is orphaned when her mother dies of an overdose, and is forced to leave her life as a pre-teen hooker on the streets of New York and relocate to live with her Grandfather in the Alps. The carnivorous, cheese-making Grandfather, convincingly played by Ted Kaczynski, tries to blend Heidi into his unnaturally happy life in the alps. The sense of dread and loathing is overwhelming as winter sets in, and Heidi tries to come to grips with the inevitable choice between death by starvation and eating goat cheese. Heidi briefly finds some comfort with Peter the goatherd, who is using the goat herding as a cover for his real business as an international hitman. Peter helps Grandfather construct a bomb to detonate in the village church on Christmas Eve. A complicated love triangle develops involving Heidi, Peter, and the goats. At tag line at the end of the credits will assure a horrified audience that no actual goat cheese was eaten in the making of this film.

My personal favorite of the season is the Sundance re-make of *It's a Wonderful Life*. This deep psychological drama is presented with new insights into the workings of the twisted mind of bank clerk George Bailey, and the terrible domestic violence at his home. George, overcome with guilt at the oppression wrought by white males against all other life forms, decides to take all of the money in the Savings and Loan and give it to a group home for Lesbian women of color to fund their cottage industries program. There is little or no chance for repayment, and when depositors find out, it starts a run on the bank, led by heterosexual white males. When they demand their money from the bank, George instead gives them uni-sex caftans made from organic, un-bleached cotton sewn at the group home.

George is fired from his job and takes up serious drinking. The already violent domestic scene gets worse, and his wife gets a restraining order. George is about to hit rock bottom when he is rescued by a heroine dealer named Clarence. Clarence assures George that every time a bell rings, some junkie scores a really good hit.

The bank's depositors, not satisfied with the clothes sewn in the sustainable cottage industries run by the Lesbian women of color group home, begin to hound George and threaten his life. In that well remembered final scene, George's supporters come forward and donate funds to pay for a sex change operation that will allow George to escape the wrath of the white male oppressors. A tag line in the credits will assure a somewhat disappointed audience that no heterosexual white males were injured in the making of this film.

There was a re-make of *The Sound of Music* later that night, but I just didn't have the heart to go see it. It focuses on the sordid affair between the telegram delivery boy and Mother Superior.

January 25, 1997

SUNDANCE WRAP-UP

This is ordinarily the column where I rant and rave about what a pain in the backside the Sundance Film Festival is. You've heard it all before, and unless you have been down with the flu, you've probably lived the event all by yourself. So I'll let the opportunity go by with only a few of my favorite Sundance Moments:

This may be the quintessential Sundance experience. I was in the Deli getting lunch. The place was packed with the usual black-garbed film types, with their film festival credential passes hanging around their necks like crucifixes. The din of cell phones ringing was overwhelming as they communicated with the nether world and summoned up the prince of darkness. Here I was in a setting as familiar as my own living room (I've eaten lunch there a couple of times a week for better than 15 years), and nothing computes. I've stumbled into some Satanic Ritual. So I get to the front of the line to place my order, and the guy in front of me orders his lunch: A chocolate chip cookie and a platter of onion rings.

The next day, I saw Bob Redford himself. He was right there on Main Street, cleverly disguised as an overstuffed chair upholstered in a bold southwestern print. He was not wearing black, nor talking on the cell phone. His posse all wore black and all were on the phone. Some were on two phones at once. But there he was.

I decided to try an experiment with Film Festival. For the last couple of years, I've just avoided going to town during the event that makes "Park City buzz like New York" (which is, of course, the problem). This year, I tried to infiltrate the belly of the beast. I dressed in Film Festival fashion, as best I could. Black turtleneck, a black fleece vest, a black baseball hat, black wrap-around sun glasses, and a three day growth of beard (that isn't quite as black as it was 10 years ago). I went to Main Street, and blended in. People I've known for years walked right by me without recognition, some actually rolling their eyes.

I was getting free coffee from the Starbucks people. In fact, it was hard to walk more than a few paces without somebody sticking a free cup of coffee in my hand. Frankly, I think there ought to be a law against giving these amped-up coastal types anything with caffeine in it. This is an event that doesn't require stimulants, but I scored my free latte, and walked the street.

Before long, I was into the spirit of the event, kicking dogs and snarling at children, and trying to sell my film. That was quite strange, because I didn't even know I had made a film to sell, but you never know. Just in case, I grabbed a video cassette out of the drawer at random, and went out to find a market.

My film was unique. It was produced by my cousin the last year we were in the cattle business. It was a marketing video of the cattle. The idea was that we could send a video of the steers to several livestock auctions cheaper than we could freight the actual steers. If they are in Omaha and don't sell, well, you can't afford to freight them back home. So the video seemed like the way to try several markets. The cattle buyers could look at the video and get an idea about how the steers looked on the hoof. I guess an experienced cattle buyer can see them on the hoof and imagine them on the hook or on the old Charm-glo grill.

Anyway, the film is about the steers. The plot is pretty thin. They don't sing or dance, or anything like that. There's no synchronized swimming. They just walk in front of the camera, giving that "I Wish I Was an Oscar Meyer Wiener" smile, and strutting their stuff. About forty minutes of that. It's pretty boring, but also kind of hypnotic. If you've seen one Hereford steer, you've seen them all. But, much to my surprise, it was a big success. I've got two deals in the works for national distribution. I had to hire an agent and everything. Who knows what it will look like when the special effects people are through with it. We're hoping to avoid the PG rating, but it's hard to get enough sex and violence for an R with a movie starring a bunch of neutered cattle. That's the magic of Film Festival. Nothing makes a bit of sense, and everybody takes it so seriously.

August 11, 1994

DECAFFEINATED BEES

The 26th annual Park City Art Festival is only a year away, so it's none too soon to start planning your parking strategy for the big event. That is, assuming that there is a 26th. Reverend Henry Camping is still holding to his prediction that the world will end in a flash of fire this September. He's even narrowed the dates down a little better. Before he used to just say "September" and leave us wondering. I had sort of put my bets on the Equinox. But now the Reverend has said the big event will fall between the 6th to the 15th. That pretty much means that non-profit organizations trying to get a food booth permit for next year's Art Festival need to look at other avenues for fund raising.

It's hard to believe that there have been 25 Art Festivals. I've been to almost all of them. I missed the first, and there were a couple in there at other intervals, but for the last 13 years, I've been there in a Coke booth pouring sodas. It's been a good experience on the whole. A friend pointed out the other day that a significant amount of self-righteousness can be bought for just a few hours of community volunteer work.

I've enjoyed being a volunteer soda jerk all these years. It's a great reinforcement of career decisions that steered away from anything having to do with the food and beverage business. Three or four hours of selling Cokes to a hot, demanding public is enough to last a whole year. If I had to deal with it every day, there would be hot coffee "spilled" on more than a few deserving folks.

The Coke booth is also a great vantage point for people watching. I'm holed up in the shade, lots of ice and cold drinks, and safely out of range of strollers, umbrellas, walking sticks, sixty pound purses, cigars, and other weapons of mass destruction people wield in close quarters. The parade just marches by.

Selling Cokes is a way to get in touch with the latest social trends among that class of trend-setters that I normally don't run into living out in Woodland. It was at Art Festival a few years ago that I first saw a pierced nipple. A guy came up to the counter and ordered a drink, and all I could say was, "Excuse me, but there's a safety pin stuck in your nipple." The aching in my chest was almost enough to call the EMT's. His girlfriend, whose hardware collection was just slightly out of sight, seemed to think it was pretty cool.

Over the years, tattoos have made a bit of a comeback. What used to be the mark of Marines with drinking problems has now found wide acceptance among ordinary teenagers with drinking problems. Some folks have turned themselves into walking murals. I understand a new fashion statement working its way West is corporate logo tattoos. What better way to make a good first impression than to have Ford Motor or Husqverna Chainsaw's logo tattooed on your neck. Maybe next year.

The Coke booth alternates between Dr. Pepper one year and some kind of orange the next. This was the orange year, and the Diet Dr. Pepper people knew it and stayed home. There is a look about Diet Dr. Pepper people appearing at the counter that gives them away. I can spot the Diet Dr. Pepper drinkers from a block away. They have Dr. Pepper eyes.

The people watching this year was not up to its usual standard. I got an early shift in a bad location. My Coke wagon was hidden behind the deep freezer where all the ice for the Art Festival was stored. They go through a lot of ice, and it's a big freezer. Not many people ventured behind the freezer to buy a drink from me this year. Those who did looked pretty conventional. There was one nose ring, but that's about it for exotic hardware.

It was so slow that I had to amuse myself watching bees instead of people this year. The bees were swarming around the spigots on the Coke machine. They really liked the stuff, except for the Diet Coke, which they didn't seem to care for. But the Real Thing was just what they had in mind.

All insects are a little creepy to me, and the ones that can kill you if enough of them sting you are especially bad, when there are more than enough of them buzzing around. I worked out a kind of accommodation, giving them one Coke machine, while I worked from the other, but I still wanted a bee keeper's suit to feel comfortable. They really liked the Coke. If you think ordinary bees are aggressive, try loading them up on sugar and caffeine.

These were wired bees with jangled nerves and a bad attitude. They were extremely alert bees who kept shouting, "Please, I'd rather do it myself." They hovered around the handles on the spigots, and formed squadrons that dive-bombed like they were going to fly up the leg of my shorts. One landed on the counter and jittered while lapping up a drop of spilled Coke. It was pathetic. The hive will be buzzing well into October. Having experienced them both ways, I think I prefer decaffeinated bees.

I walked the street after my shift, looking at the artwork. There were some nice things this year. A couple of my favorite artists were sold out. I like the carved wooden toys, and was all ready to buy the tractor/manure spreader combination, but he was sold out. I got a wind sock that looks like it will scare away the woodpeckers that are stripping the siding off my house. It's been a banner year for woodpeckers, and they are thick around here. This wind sock spins and flutters, and ought to scare them away.

It bothered the artist that I was buying the wind sock for such a utilitarian purpose. It was, after all, art. His whimsical spirit, reflected in the carefully crafted wind sock, was supposed to cheer and entertain. It wasn't supposed to have any function-- it's art. Then I come along and tell him I buy one every year to scare the devil out of woodpeckers; that I didn't care about the colors of the wind sock any more than I care about the color of the handle on a new hammer.

These artists have ways of communicating with each other, and I received a pretty cold reception at every booth I visited after that. They gave me a look that said, "Yeah, we heard all about you. You're not buying any of *my* pottery to scare woodpeckers away." Maybe next year.

January 19, 1995

GAY SENATORS' FILM FESTIVAL

The skiing has been so good lately that it's been hard to keep up on current events around town. The promotions for the KPCW fund raiser have started already, which means there are only about 330 shopping days left until Christmas. Hidden in the middle of the media blitz on the fund raiser, there is the school district's special election. They are looking for voter approval for an additional property tax for computers and stuff, and then the $30 million for the new schools and more stuff. Debate on that one hasn't really heated up yet. Over at the Castle, things are so slow these days that the City Council is only meeting once in January, and even with the new commissioners, the county is pretty quiet, just the sound of resumes being sent out.

But the skiing has been amazing. I've had my head so deep in the powder that I may have missed a some things the last few days. For example, the other day while I was driving over to town, the radio was cutting in and out like it does in the mountains. I was listening for a ski report and weather forecast, and not paying a whole lot attention to the news. In one of those interviews with the Chamber of Commerce people, it sounded like there was a pretty unusual special event going on. I didn't pay all that much attention at the time, but unless I'm seriously confused, I'm sure that the Chamber was announcing that Park City played host to the Gay Senator's Film Festival last week.

47

In an effort to get more efficient, the special events promoters at the Chamber have begun to consolidate events (a suggestion you first read about here, by the way). Rather than tediously promoting one special group after another, the Chamber is lumping them all together into more manageable affairs. At least I think that is the theory behind last week's Gay Senators' Film Festival. Get it all over with at once.

"Senators' Cup" has been a regular event for a long time. The event is a charity fund raiser for the Primary Children's Hospital in Salt Lake. Each year, big corporations and lobbyists make generous donations to pay medical bills for sick children in exchange for a weekend to hobnob with the Senators where they make sure they don't have to provide health insurance for the kids' parents. That is not to say that these same big corporations wouldn't make the same donation to the hospital in exchange for a bowl of Jell-O served in the hospital cafeteria, and a weekend of mop hockey with the cleaning staff. It's just more fun to make the contribution in a context where they get to personally discuss with the United States Senate the importance of certain tax exemptions, low minimum wages, and on and on.

Last year, one of the tabloid television shows did an extremely negative story on the Senators' Cup, painting it as big money buying secret access to political power instead of a benefit for crippled children. Imagine that. Anyway, after that, I wasn't too surprised to see Senators' Cup go underground this year. There was almost no publicity of the event, and I only knew it was happening because a friend of mine is one of the lobbyist types who always comes out to make his pitch to the senators. Not that they aren't all dear personal friends who he wanted to spend the best powder weekend of the decade with, skiing on First Time, and talking about mind-numbing public policy issues.

Underground, yes, but I was surprised that Senators' Cup was in the closet. Yet there it was, deep in the ski report: a quiet welcome to the members of the United States Senate and Gay

48

Community skiing Park City this week. Those AIDS ribbons were showing up all over town in the windows of the politically correct merchants. I had no idea so many members of the Senate were gay. Does Jesse Helms know about this? First the Navy, and now right there in the halls of Congress. This Clinton guy has got to go.

Last year, there was a big gay ski event here. Depending on whose trademark lawyer you talked to, it was called either "Gay Ski Week" or "Winterfest." I'm not sure how many people showed up, but the publicity for it was big, and the controversy was out of control. There were nasty letters to the editor from people who didn't want their condo rented to "them" and on and on. It got pretty ugly.

So this year, somebody wisely made the decision to hold whatever event they wanted to hold without a lot of fanfare. Don't ask; don't tell; don't care. It drew about as much attention as a convention of orthodontists from Kansas, or, for that matter, the Senators.

Invisibly staging the two events in the same week was brilliant. If anybody really cared, say you are on a chair lift and look at the guy with the really expensive hair cut sitting next to you and wonder, and are crass enough to ask, "Are you one of *them*?" the person on the chair has the option of answering any number of ways, including, "Goodness, no. I'd never run for public office."

Maybe we have reached a new level of maturity in our resort town development. There is something really nice about having special events or high profile groups in town, and being able to more or less ignore them. They do their thing, and the rest of us do ours, and it's not a big deal. I know the real estate interests were snuggled up with the Senators to protect the income tax deduction for second home mortgage interest, but the rest of us hardly noticed, except when we paid our tax bill. That's a tender topic right now, since those of us who are self employed just had to cough up our 4th quarter estimated income taxes.

I love the notion that we are going to push teenage mothers with infants off welfare--and into jobs paying upwards of $4.25 an hour--because it costs too much to support them, but we are not about to take away the public subsidy of million dollar second homes by eliminating the interest deduction from the owner's taxes. Maybe if those teenage mothers got together and sponsored a ski vacation for members of the Senate, where they could lobby for their cause, and suggest that $4.25 an hour isn't an adequate wage to support a gerbil, let alone a single parent household, they might change things.

The single teenage mothers suffer from a weak lobbyist. There's no way members of Congress would talk about owners of million dollar second homes in ski resorts the way they talk about unwed teenage mothers. But then, if those teenage mothers had life organized to the point of hiring better lobbyists (the National Sisterhood of Unwed Teenage Mothers), they probably would have been organized enough to avoid being teenage mothers in the first place, and deductibility of second home mortgage interest might mean more to them. Let them eat cake.

Chapter 3

Living
in the
Mountains

February 15, 1990

LIGHT IN THE CALF SHED

From my bedroom window I can look across the river, then a wide pasture, and see my neighbors' barnyard area. Although it's quite a distance, I can see the daytime activity there as they come and go with feed wagons and trucks. At night, there is usually just the moonlight on the snow. The other night, though, I woke up late and noticed lights in one of the buildings. My neighbor is a pretty detail-minded sort, and does not just forget to turn lights off. Lights in the calf sheds mean spring is on the way.

My neighbors, a father and son partnership, raise beef. Some of their cows, the older and more experienced ones, are out on the desert in southern Utah. They have their calves there by themselves. The first-timers spend the winter here on the ranch, and give birth in nests of clean straw and sawdust in the shed whose light I can see from my window. In the morning, while they feed the rest of the cows in the pasture, they check to see which ones are getting close to dropping their calves. My neighbor explained all the outward signs to me once, in greater detail than I really cared to know.

The cows who are ready get moved from the pasture to the calf sheds where they are warm and dry for the delivery. Whenever there is a cow (or sometimes as many as a half dozen) in the shed, the neighbors keep watch like expectant fathers in the waiting room. They have a two hour schedule, taking turns checking on the cows. Sometimes, a cow having her first calf will have trouble with the delivery. The tools range from a kind of block-and-tackle forceps to a tractor when

53

a breech birth threatens the life of the cow. Other times, a first-time mother cow will be frightened by the presence of the calf, or won't figure out that she needs to lick the covering off so the calf can breathe. They seldom lose one when they keep a close watch.

The calf shed is a couple of hundred yards from their houses, so the nightly calf checks require getting dressed, it is February after all, and trudging out through the snow. Ten, twelve, two, four, six, then off and on through the day. The calves seem to be born at night most of the time. Technology could help with this process. We have talked about rigging up a home video camera in the calf shed. They could hit the remote control on the tv, and make their rounds without even getting out of bed, let alone pulling on boots and coats. It could be done that way, and in a lot of places, I suppose it is. But not here.

My neighbors would never admit it, but I think they actually like getting up several times in the dead of night to go check their cows in sub-zero temperatures. The anxiousness of the mother-to-be, who knows something is happening to her, but, never having been through it before, isn't sure what--is something that can't be captured on camera. They actually give a little comfort to the cows, checking in now and then. They would be embarrassed to install a sound system, so they could broadcast a few soothing words from the house-- admitting that they talk to their cows. But I know that those cold night visits to the calf shed are not without a little conversation. Even a song or two wouldn't surprise me. Cows are nowhere near as stupid as they look. They appreciate a kind word and a soft voice.

With the kind of cedar-barked cowboy toughness you might expect, my neighbors say the night watch is purely economic, to cut their losses from the first year, high risk births. That may be partly true, but I get a sense that they feel a duty to be there when the cow needs them. These cows provide them with a pretty good living, all things considered, and fairness and respect require that they provide the cows with a pretty good life, despite the inevitable conclusion. Television cameras, tape recorded music, and lots of other modern devices may come close to doing the whole job, but the dignity of the occasion really dictates that they be there in person, ready to do whatever needs to be done.

Every year at this season, I say I will sit through the night with one of the cows to witness the wet, messy, miracle of birth. I never do it. It is always too cold, or I have places to be the next day and can't function on a sleepless night. I also wonder if I would be intruding, standing there watching with no ability to help. The beef I deal with is mostly in Saran Wrap, and the cow would know it. I don't belong there. So instead, when I wake up in the night, I look out the window to see if the light is on in the calf shed, signaling that there is at least one cow there waiting her time. I wish her well, and think of my neighbors, one or the other of them (and if the truth is told, usually both, despite their arrangement of alternating checks) sitting there on a bale of hay, in the corner out of the wind, watching the simplest and most complex elements of life.

There aren't a lot of places you can live and watch a miracle happen outside your window almost every night, and have it be so common that you don't get up to watch it. The cows are only one of several around here. There is the cyclical rise and fall of the river, seasonal and daily as the sun melts the snow. Within a only a few weeks, there will be crops growing in the fields, and robins on the beam above the front porch, and aspen leaves growing so fast you can almost see it happen.

This talk of spring is maybe rushing the season a little bit. This week is almost always the coldest weather of the season. There's no mistaking it for June. But maybe that's why I like to look out the window at night and see the warm glow of the light in the calf shed across the river. If the calves are dropping, spring can't be far away.

October 19, 1995

REPAIRING THE BARN

The trees are almost bare out in my neighborhood. The wind the last few days stirred up a blizzard of leaves and stripped the trees. The ground is covered with leaves, and in the mornings, when there is a little frost on the ground, they are slick as cartoon banana peels. There is a beaver working in the stream behind my house, and I have to pull the dam every morning or the yard gets flooded. In just the last couple of weeks, the sun has shifted south, and now rises in a different notch in the mountains than it did a month ago.

A couple of afternoons this week, I've been able to sit out on the porch with the sun hitting me and the heat radiating off the house and just soak it all in. The ski magazines are coming, and there's something kind of nice reading them on the porch, watching the season change. It's a great time of year, unless you are a building contractor. There are a lot of construction sites where they are working on borrowed time already. Deer Valley's expanded Snow Park Lodge is still without a roof. It will take a miracle to have it in "Deer Valley condition" by December.

I've got things in reasonable condition around my place for winter, though I could always cut a little more fire wood. My neighbors have a wood pile as big as their house, and that always makes me worry a little. Do they know something about the coming winter that I don't? They are retired and able to keep a fire going all day, so they more or less heat their house with the wood stove. They go through a little more wood than I do, just burning a fire at night but relying on the furnace most of the time. Their house is also nearly a hundred years old, and maybe not as well insulated as mine.

I've never had the nerve to stop and count the farm outbuildings around here. It would be too discouraging, because all of them are in need of work. Last year, we did a major repair on the old sheep barn. This year, we got a pretty good start on the dairy barn. It's almost a twin to the Osguthorpe barn. They were built at about the same time, in the early 1930's, and may have been built by the same people.

The lumber for ours was cut right on the ranch, and milled with a portable saw mill. It's all big, rough cut material, and nailed together with huge nails. The labor involved in building it must have been amazing. One wall has rotted at the bottom, and fallen off the foundation in places. The whole building sagged in the middle, and was about 8 inches lower than it was supposed to be.

So we've jacked it up and put a new bottom plate on the foundation and new studs in the wall. It's more or less up to square again and seems solid. There is the problem of a gap almost a foot wide between the bottom of the siding on the walls and the floor. It really needs to be stripped off and new siding put on, but for this year, getting the basic frame back on the foundation before there is snow on the roof is a good beginning.

It's a great old barn. It doesn't serve much purpose any more. No cows live in the bottom floor. The loft used to be stacked full of hay. We don't winter any cattle here now, so there is no reason to fill it. What little hay the horses eat is stacked in a more convenient location, saving the labor of lifting the hay into and then out of the loft.

The guy helping me has worked on the ranch for years. He's older than the barn, and sort of remembers it being built when he was just a kid. When he was in high school, his father

58

worked for the people we bought the place from, and he would work on the hay crew in the summers. He described the process of hauling the hay into the loft with the pulleys hanging from the track in the roof, with one set of ropes to lift the hay bales up, and another rope to move the load along the center axis of the barn to drop it in the center. He rode a Belgian draft horse back and forth in the yard, pulling the hay trolley in and out of the barn while they loaded it. By the time I came along, we had an electric conveyor belt that would run bales from the ground up into the loft, and a second one that lifted it to the top of the stack. Even that was hard work. Originally, I guess the hay went in loose rather than baled, with big forks hanging from the trolley.

The barn creaks and groans as we jack it up. We can only raise it a few inches at a time, then block that area up and raise it someplace else, working up and down the wall in increments of about ten feet. The barn cats hiss and run outside, and the dust from 60 years of hay falls through the cracks in the floor from the empty loft above. Haunta virus crosses my mind, though the more immediate threat is one of the posts falling off the jack and bashing me in the head.

Some of the other buildings are probably better dealt with by letting the snow cave them in, then carting the rubble away. They all had a purpose once, and somebody built each one to address a specific need. There was a reason for the proportions of the door, the placement of the windows, and where the building was built in relation to the others. Through the years, the modifications are pretty easy to see--a widened door for a bigger swather, the entry cut taller for different equipment, a doorway blocked off because the milking shed was now a machine shop.

It's hard to find a use for the barn now. It's too hard to get anything into the loft, and the stalls are designed around the proportions of milk cows, and don't accommodate tractors, cars, or other equipment that should be under cover. The ceiling is pretty low. I guess cows don't need a lot of overhead clearance, and every inch of additional ceiling height was that much more height the hay had to be hoisted. There is a real thrift in the design of the barn, both in its construction and the way it operated.

The other day, while we were taking a break and discussing the next step in the process, I mentioned the nearly new, million dollar, house in American Flag that is being torn down to make way for a bigger house on the lot. My helper, who lives in the same house his father was born in, didn't believe me. He thought I was making it up. Nobody would tear down a new house.

He wants to re-build the mangers and stalls we had to tear out to get access to the wall.

August 3, 1995

OUT STANDING IN HIS FIELD

The other day, I saw something I've never seen before. A cow moose and her calf were standing in the pasture, and the calf was nursing. It was pretty early in the morning and I was out turning irrigation water in the field. The morning was cold, and there was frost on the grass and ice at the edges of the pools of water left by the irrigation. The moose were out in the middle of the field, standing broadside to the sun, warming up. The cow saw me, decked out in mis-matched sweat pants and sweat shirt, rubber boots, and my trusty shovel. She didn't seem to care a lot, but I also wasn't very close.

The horses had that wigged-out look they get when anything unusual is afoot. They were in the opposite end of the pasture, with their butts against the fence, staring off in the general direction of the moose. There have been enough moose through here in the last several years that I would expect the horses to be used to them by now. They've adapted to farm machinery, highway construction equipment, dogs, crying babies, ATVs, and a Republican Congress, but a moose will still send the horses into a full equine panic.

I watched the moose while I moved the canvas dam down the ditch to water another part of the field, and leaned on the shovel for a minute to see if they would turn around. The calf was on the far side, behind its mother. When it tried to move to the other side, for the second course of breakfast, the mother turned around, keeping the calf more or less hidden from view. I decided to go back to the house before getting her too upset.

There are few measurable rewards from running a farm in this climate. It snows in June, freezes in July, dries up in August, just in time for the snow in September. And people are surprised that farmers and ranchers aren't raking in the money. But it's hard to put a price on watching the moose family eat breakfast in the morning.

I've spent a fair amount of time irrigating this summer. We have a full time guy who waters the hay fields 6 days a week. He's the best there is at it, and people say he can make water run up hill just by giving it a crusty look. On his day off, we hired a high school kid. He's good, but things keep coming up. He made it into the national high school rodeo championships (I was thinking of getting Tonya Harding to pay a visit to his horse), the SAT exam, a family vacation that had been planned a long time before, football stuff, and one Saturday, he had to "show his pigs." I didn't even ask what that was all about.

Anyway, I've ended up doing the relief irrigation about half the summer. It's a lot of work. We have five different streams running all the time. A canvas dam (which is really plastic these days, but they are still called canvas dams) across the ditch spills the water out in the field. In some places, it will run to the end of the field in about a half hour. In other areas, the ground is so well drained that it can run in the same spot most of the day and not reach the end of the field.

When the water gets to the end of the field, it's time to move the dam upstream about 10 to 20 feet to start the process again, flooding strip after strip until the whole field has been soaked. Then you switch the water into the next ditch to start on the next piece.

I wear knee high boots. The full time guy has hip waders that he has to fold up and down every time he gets in or out of the truck. No matter what boots you have, my experience has been that sooner or later, they will be filled with water that only yesterday was snow. The old school of thought is that you just tough it out, and finish the day with your legs wet and numb from the cold. My approach is to wear the boots until they get swamped, then switch over to sneakers and shorts. My legs get a little scratched up walking through the deep hay, but at least my lips aren't blue.

Something about irrigation fascinates me. It's probably a genetic predisposition, descending from farmers on both sides of the family. My grandfather on my father's side was said to irrigate a field until the fence posts started growing. My grandfather on mom's side irrigated a smaller farm, but also had a dry farm in Idaho. Dry farming is a lot of work, and maybe more risky, but because there isn't irrigation, it always seemed like dry farmers were getting away with something. I didn't realize at the time that there were millions of acres of farm land that actually produced crops on the basis of natural rainfall alone.

Funny things happen out there in the fields. With the water on one area, there will be gopher holes squirting like geysers in the middle of a lower field. Fish swim down stream until they hit the canvas dam, then shoot back up the ditch, to the main canal, and maybe all the way back up to the river. My dog likes to "surf" in the ditches when I pull the dam and send a surge of water downstream to the next location.

Between turns, I was sitting in the truck reading the mail. There was a brochure on a stress management clinic, where, for $300 bucks, some expert would teach you relaxation techniques, meditation, exercises, and time management skills that were guaranteed to make life blissful. The clinic was to be held in a windowless hotel conference room, under fluorescent lights, with validated parking available. Lunch on your own in some fine hotel coffee shop.

I got thinking that there were opportunities here. Maybe I could offer stress management clinics out here in the hay field, where for $300 bucks, stressed out business people, lawyers, and other yuppies on the edge of cardiac arrest could spend a day turning water, listening to country western classics on the truck radio, and watching sand hill cranes hunt for bugs in the soaked up fields. They would have to be frisked for cellular phones first.

I could package the whole thing up with some meditation training tapes (mostly old Patsy Kline songs), a souvenir shovel, a pair of hip waders with a painted on logo, and maybe a t-shirt with the sleeves cut off to complete the package. By the end of the day, they would be munching of a piece of grass, watching the shadows for the return of the cow moose.

October 18, 1997

GRAVEL POLITICS

Local politics are beginning to heat up. I'm not talking about Park City and the election that nobody seems to care much about. The primary was pretty predictable. Brad Olch got 50% of the vote, which is exactly the number of people who didn't get building permits during his last term in office. Niki Lowery got roughly 30% of the vote, which represents the number of people who have had the pleasure of dealing with City Hall, and voted "no." J. B. Nelmark got a surprising 20% of the vote. I think that represents the number of people who can't afford building permits, and are having a really good time.

So now it moves into the finals, and aside from little forays into delicate issues of racism, the campaign seems to be settling back into a discussion of parking meters and buses. Yawn. On the race issue, the fact is that none of the candidates is a racist, and the problems are well beyond the scope of local government to address. The federal government hasn't found a solution to immigration issues in 200 years. It seems unlikely that anybody at City Hall is going to find the answer. It's probably healthy to be talking about it, and at least being aware that there are some tensions that probably can be massaged away. But let's not have an election based on who thinks their opponent is the biggest bigot. They're not.

On the other hand, I think Park City as a whole is pretty suspicious of anybody with a household income that isn't well into six figures, regardless of ethnicity. That we might work on a little more.

No, the politics that have become complicated are right in my neighborhood. We're graveling the roads in preparation for winter. Graveling the roads is an art. If you do it too early in the season, kids on those damn ATV's will roar down the lane at super-sonic speeds, sending rooster tails of expensive gravel into the trees. If you do it too late, the roads are already muddy, and the dump trucks sink in. We get gravel, but it is all in foot deep tire ruts. If the road isn't slightly soggy, though, the gravel doesn't work in, and the first snow plowing pushes it all off to the side where it will chew up the big snow blower.

This year the technical aspect of it was complicated by the fact that every dump truck in this end of the world has been pressed into service hauling asphalt to pave the new Tabiona Turnpike over Wolf Creek Pass. This is part of a federal welfare program for highway contractors, and they have been working for about 4 years now building a super highway connecting Woodland with Tabiona. It is important enough to merit about $20 million in federal funds, but not important enough to plow the snow on. In fact, Utah's highway people want to abandon it to the counties.

The problem of coordinating gravel deliveries on our neighborhood dirt roads with the whims of the weather and highway construction has been a bit of a problem. That's the easy part.

The owners association that is paying for the gravel has limited funds, so there is never enough money to do the whole thing at once. Instead, each year we pick a couple of areas that seem especially bad and put gravel there until the money runs out. The problem is that the worst areas always seem to be the same places. That's because the traffic is heaviest there (we're talking about an alarming five or six cars a day in some places). Other areas are sort of soft, and no matter how much gravel gets dumped there, it is swallowed into the center of the earth the next week. Overall, the roads are more or less passable in the winter.

But the gravel always ends up in front of the same houses. Some people don't get gravel in front of their places for years at a time, and others have a fresh layer every fall. Some people who pay their assessments don't get much benefit directly in front of their houses, though they get to drive over the gravel dumped in front of other houses. Some people who don't pay their assessments get gravel in front of their houses anyway because they are in the low spots that need to be filled. I've consulted a civil engineer to see if there are ways to design the mud to swallow the cars of the deadbeats, but not those who paid their assessments.

One guy gets gravel even though he doesn't want it because he claims the road encroaches on his front yard. We have to wait until he's drained the pipes and gone back to Salt Lake for the winter before dumping gravel on his front lawn. The road encroached a little before he started whining, but since he really got on us, it is moving ever closer. If he keeps it up, there will be cars driving through his living room.

Gravel comes in a variety of colors and flavors, and everybody has an opinion. Some prefer "road base" that is gravel with a sort of clay sand mixed in with it. Once it's compacted, it's bullet proof. Until it's fully compacted, it will swallow a Ford Festiva, and pack the fenders of a 4 x 4 truck with mud. Some people like golf ball sized gravel because it drains well and seems to stay in place. Others hate it because it's like walking or riding your bike on a road covered with golf balls.

Another neighbor likes a dark, heavy material that is like UDOT uses in that chip-seal/broken windshield program. He thinks it looks like a nice paved street. It smells like sulfur when it gets wet. We mostly use a finer gravel that is just the right size to get lodged in the lug soles of your shoes. After a walk out to the mail box, it sounds like you have tap shoes on in the house.

There have been a couple of new people who suggested that we should pave the roads. That was met with general disapproval. If you want to live on a paved road, why did you buy a house on a dirt road? For that matter, why did you leave California in the first place?

The only universal rule about graveling our streets is that no matter how we do it, there will be complaints. Well, there is another almost universal rule. Within a week of graveling the roads, there will be a water line break that forces us to dig it up.

Anyway, the politics of graveling a couple of miles of dirt roads are plenty complicated. It's about all I can deal with. So I can't imagine people wanting to run for office so they can deal with the more complicated politics of running a whole city government. We can make a lot of people angry on a budget that is less than the City spends on paper clips. I'm convinced that spending more would only make things worse.

So I'm perfectly content to get by on un-paved roads with a little gravel in the low spots, and leave the big problems to somebody else. Though we are looking at installing parking meters.

February 1, 1996

THE BLIZZARD OF '96

So, have you had enough snow yet? This is sort of getting out of hand. For the last three weeks, the average snow fall every day has got to be close to a foot, and there have been a couple of those two footers in there, with hurricane force winds just to make it interesting. The skiing has been great, and there have been several of those impromptu snow holidays where people started canceling appointments, re-arranging work schedules, and basically closing up shop to take advantage of it.

Years ago, that was just kind of understood. We didn't have a lot of commuters or non-skiers living in Park City, and so closing down business for a powder holiday was just automatic. The reaction this year was a little different, with newcomers saying things like "You mean you can do that? I can call my boss in Salt Lake and say I'm going skiing?" Well, there are some finer points to be worked on in the excuse category, but yes, you can do that. And probably should more often.

It's unusual for me to say anything nice about UDOT, but I've really got to hand it to the guys running the plows. Despite storms on a Biblical scale, the roads have mostly been open, clear, and in remarkable shape. I saw one of the drivers the other day in the gas station/bakery/junk food outlet in Kamas, and he didn't look anywhere near as good as the roads. I think they are operating on about 4 hours' sleep, fueled by gallons of coffee and doughnuts by the tons. I hope they get a little break now and then. They have done a great job.

There are little inconveniences, and anybody can find a street or intersection that is a real mess, but by and large, the snowplow drivers from UDOT, Summit County, and Park City have worked miracles.

Snow plowing is something I'm getting more familiar with by the hour. The lane to my house is a little dirt road. Everybody else with a house on it has the good sense to pack off to Arizona for the winter, so I have to plow the whole thing. Once it gets started, my old Dodge, (also known as the Zamboni or the Red Death), does a pretty good job clearing snow. The starting process involves squirting ether into the air cleaner, sticking a one inch bolt into the choke to block it open, and recitation of the same incantation Karl Malone says before taking a foul shot.

If all goes well, the ether will explode and blow the bolt out of the carburetor, allowing the choke to close at the critical moment of ignition. It has to stay choked for about a nanosecond until the carburetor vacuum is strong enough to hold the choke open again before the engine floods and stalls out. It involves crawling in and out of the engine on a truck that stands about 4 feet high at the fender, all in a garage that is only inches wider than the truck itself. This is called an automatic choke, and Chrysler equipped all their vehicles with it because it was considered easier than pulling a knob on the dash board to operate a manual choke. More often than not, it also involves jumper cables and pacts with the devil to get the Zamboni started and to keep it running long enough to get the road pushed open. It's a fine piece of machinery.

This year, the snow has come faster than the Zamboni can push it, even running the plow several times a day. I've spent hours on the farm tractor with a blower on the back, blasting the windrows of snow back. It's kind of fun, until a low branch turns the nozzle around and I get hit with 90 horsepower of blowing snow right in the face. It was about the same feeling you get up skiing on a couple of those "wind hold" days.

Before we got the 4 wheel drive John Deere tractor, my uncle used to try to keep the place open with a Ford 8N. For those of you who grew up in deprived conditions and aren't conversant with antique tractors, the Ford 8N was a great little tractor for small farms. It was about World War II vintage, if not before. It did a lot of things very well, but the idea of plowing open all the roads on the ranch with a Ford 8N is about like being handed a 19" wide Toro lawn mower and facing a golf course of knee deep grass. It worked, but I think plowing snow must have been a full time job.

I was putting the John Deere back in the shed where we keep it, and plugging in the block heater for the night. This time of year, we pamper it like a Ferrari. My uncle was there, and we got talking about his days on the Ford 8N. He said what he really wondered about was the generation before him, when the little Ford would have looked like the space shuttle by comparison to coping with winter on horseback. In deep snow, it would have been a pretty good day's ride to get down the canyon to Woodland. A trip all the way to Kamas would have been an epic journey in conditions like this. I guess the only thing you could do is hunker down for the winter and call for pizza delivery.

The tightly compacted lay out of Old Town makes a lot of sense in a season like this when the only sure means of transportation is on foot.

We've been shoveling the roofs on the farm outbuildings, digging out the mail boxes, and getting cars stuck at a record pace for three weeks now, and it's pretty clear we're losing the battle. The forecasters had promised a break on Tuesday, but it was another foot of snow. When it's man against nature, nature always wins. It's good to be reminded who's in charge every now and then. The overall snow depth is not all that unusual, but I had bare ground in my yard on January 15th. The fences are buried now. I had to use ski pole probes to find the propane tank, the wood pile and the dog house. There is a

71

cornice on my roof that hangs out a good 4 feet. I've never had to do avalanche control work in the back yard before.

The force of these storms has been great to watch. A couple of nights, I've turned on the yard lights and sat by the window just watching it snow. The storms are unique. There was one that blew in from the east, another that had big flakes, some that have come horizontal, and even one that came straight down. It's beautiful.

Keep skiin', shovelin', and smilin'. When this all melts off sometime in August we will be survivors of the winter of '96.

[Note: In the middle of all of this, PBS chose to run a four hour special about the Donner Party. A friend of mine who is a serious historian said it was very well done. I didn't dare watch it. I also got word that they had cancelled church one Sunday. They blamed it on the storm, but my aunt said she thought they were afraid to get that many people together at the same time until the general mood improved.]

December 14, 1996

GOLD MEDAL SNOW PLOW ACTION

I had to dig back in the old books on this one, but yes, ladies and gentlemen, we have a new record on our hands! This is the earliest in the winter that the snow plow driver has taken out my mailbox. And he did it with enough style and technique to get extra points for the degree of difficulty, with a bonus for scattering the mail clear into Wyoming.

For years, I've watched in amazement at the ability of the snow plow drivers on my route to work over a mailbox. There was a guy who was able to knock the door open, blow the mail into the river, pack the mailbox tight with snow, then actually re-close the door and put the flag up, all without leaving the truck or even slowing down. Now that is skill acquired over many years of practice.

The loss of the mailbox is an annual event. I didn't keep track of the dates at first, but over the last several years, I've recorded the date that the mailbox was rendered unusable. I normally make it until April. Back in about 1987 they got it over Thanksgiving. The driver clipped the post off at ground level, moved a bridge abutment, and knocked out phone service for a week. But that had to go into the record book as a big "DQ" because the driver lost control of the truck on a patch of ice and made physical contact between the truck and the mailbox. He was a rookie that year, but went on to the major leagues.

The score on this year's box was pretty spectacular. When snow plow driving becomes an Olympic event, this is the

73

gold medal winner and CNN's "Play of the Day." My mailbox is on one of those "L" shaped frames made of pipe, with the box hanging from chains to give it a little free play when the snow plow heaves a ton of slush its way. Normally, that is enough, and over the course of the winter, the pounding gradually mashes the arched mailbox into a piece of flat metal, but it isn't physically removed from the post.

This year, it went with a little more style. The plow hit it so hard that it blew the rivets right out of the mailbox, twisted the "L" post half way around and bent it over sideways. The only thing left was one of the chains it used to hang by. It looked like a Christmas card from the Unabomber had been opened early. What makes it more amazing is that the neighbors' mailbox is not more than a foot away from mine, on exactly the same kind of suspension system. It escaped unscathed. I can't feel bad about replacing it under circumstances like that. My only regret is that I didn't get to see it happen.

I probably shouldn't take it personally, though I've noticed that most of the other people in the area have mailboxes that have been around for decades. Mine is located next to a bridge, and there is a guardrail that makes it impossible for the mailman to pull off the road. So it's pretty exposed and vulnerable. I've listened to the trucks as they wind up the highway, and they actually accelerate when they get to my driveway. I've been told that is to heave the snow over the side of the bridge, and that the mailbox is only collateral damage, but I'm not sure I buy that. I think they have it written down in their Franklin Planner: "Smash Clyde's mail box."

If I can find the remains of the old one, I plan to mount it on a walnut base and give it to the Snowplow Drivers' Hall of Fame as a trophy.

In other traffic news, I was driving into town last week to dinner at a friend's house, and was surprised to see the City installing tank barricades on Park Avenue at the stop light.

There, under cover of darkness, in a pouring rain, City crews were installing a big pile of railroad ties in the middle of the street. It was a scene from the construction of the Berlin Wall. Since my friend lives right on Park Avenue, it made sense to go straight through the light and on up Park. But I was stopped by the border guards and asked to produce my papers. I told him that not even my dog has papers, but that last time I checked, Park Avenue was a public street. After some negotiation, and a modest cash payment, I was allowed to proceed through Checkpoint Charlie and south through the intersection.

This has something to do with "traffic calming," which I fear is a euphemism for all kinds of terrible things, including the Balkinization of Park City neighborhoods. If Park Avenue gets something that looks like a gate, everybody will want a gate. You'll need more passes and windshield decals to move from one end of Park City to the other than to cross through the Middle East. The idea is that by physically obstructing the flow of traffic at the intersection, people will be convinced to turn there, and drive on either Deer Valley or Empire, instead of Park Ave., unless their destination is 7-Eleven, the Library, or something else right on the street, in which case they will have proper travel papers.

The banner across Park Avenue that used to announce "Welcome Friends of the Friends Fund-Raiser" has been replaced with a huge blue sign that more or less says "Go Away." People who are trying to go to Main Street will be diverted, and the lower Park Avenue neighborhood will be spared having several hundred cars a day drive past their houses. Traffic will be calmed. Life will be good.

Except. Except all those cars that used to drive up Park Avenue will still be on the roads. They will still go to Main Street. They will just approach it from Deer Valley Drive through the worst intersection in town. The right turns off Heber Avenue to Main and Swede will be replaced with left turns. Traffic will stack up out to Deer Valley Drive. In the end, traffic at the Heber/Swede/Deer Valley intersection will also be calmed to the point of gridlock.

People will get out of their cars and exchange pleasantries with each other. "Hello, neighbor. It's a pleasure to meet you under these circumstances. How about moving that swell new Hummer of yours? Can I help you find a nice parking place where the sun doesn't shine?" In that traffic-calmed setting, they will sit on the hoods of their grid-locked Range Rovers sharing cappuccinos and croissants. And possibly gun fire.

The City has struggled with design on the Park Avenue tank barricade. It's hard to build a big planter in the middle of the street and have it look natural and tasteful. This is partly because, for hundreds of years of human experience, streets have not had huge piles of rail road ties stacked in the left turn lane. Huge sums of money have been spent to remove physical obstructions. People don't expect it to be there. So they have tacked reflectors all over it. In the dark of Monday night's storm, the reflectors didn't help much. There was nothing about the reflectors that said, "This isn't a truck in the left turn lane, it's a pile of railroad ties."

I bet somebody hit it before breakfast on Tuesday. That'll calm things down.

[Note: In fact the planter was hit by a car within 4 hours of being installed. There were no serious injuries. It's still there, still ugly, and as far as I can tell, traffic is still not calm.]

Chapter 4

The More Things Change, the More Things Change

October 18, 1990

HOIST ONE FOR THE HOLSTEINS

The big news around town is that Park City is now the happy owner of the Osguthorpe Dairy, assuming they can find a way to pay for it in the next five years. Much of the attention to this item of news has focused on the usual, tedious planning and land use considerations, and visual corridors and all that stuff. My views on the substantial social benefits gained through the strategic placement of a big pile of junk cars at the entrance to a community such as ours are well known, so I have to view the departure of the Holsteins with some skepticism, if not outright alarm. First the Holsteins, then the construction workers, who's next? It's only a matter of time before they quit selling white bread at Albertsons and get the dogs off Main Street.

There is nothing that is quite as down to earth as a road peppered with fresh cow pies. There is nothing quite as democratic as driving through it, either. The Saab or BMW takes just as much crap as the rusted out VW bus, right up to the door handles. There is nothing quite as innocent as a bunch of Holsteins chewing their cud and adding to the mountain of manure on the entrance to Park City. Dressed in their black and white, they have both an innocence and dignity about them. There is nothing devious about a Holstein.

Some narrow-minded people have found the mountain of manure objectionable, but to me, it always created a kind of symmetry with the mountains of figurative manure shoveled back and forth in other parts of town. Any discussion of day

79

care, nightly rental, traffic impacts, or ridgeline protection is kind of balanced by the pungent aroma of milk production. But, my views and fifty cents will buy a cup of coffee at the Mount Air, so what do I know. Anyway, it will be hard saying farewell to the Holsteins.

These are not just ordinary Holsteins, either. Their new life in a more sedate community will be a hard adjustment for them. These are resort Holsteins, born and bred to the fast lane and the bright lights. How can you keep them down on the farm when they've seen Paris or been to the World Cup? These are Holsteins that wear Vaurnets with Chums, and have Bogner ski suits hanging in their stalls. They have little Rosignol roosters on their headstalls, and their hay is served by farm hands who say things like, "Good morning. I'm Billy, and I will be your waiter this morning. In addition to the usual alfalfa cubes, we have a special French oat muffin that is excellent." These are cows who graze in an "entry corridor" instead of a pasture. Life just won't be the same if they have to get used to grazing in some dumb old field in Millard County.

The Osguthorpe Holsteins have achieved a certain celebrity, too, aside from their milk production which is said to be among the best in the dairy industry. When they are not on duty, the Osguthorpe Holsteins are Utah's most photographed cows, and don't think for a minute that they don't know it.

Nobody who has lived here through a ski season has missed the thrill of the rented car in front of them skidding through the on-coming lane of traffic so some tourist could jump out and catch that perfect picture of bucolic bliss: A couple of freshly coiffured Holsteins posing by the steaming stream, frost on the willows, the big white barn in the background, and the snow covered mountains with the warm glow of sunset on them. Day after day, week after week, the Osguthorpe Holsteins are getting their pictures taken. It's gone to their heads.

These Holsteins have been in some major national publications, on television, and probably even in a movie or two (I think they played a bit part in that Park City classic *The Boogins*). Now, with the sale of the farm, they will be moving to some less gentrified locale, where there is no novelty about cows at all. They will be just plain cows, like any others. Nobody will take their pictures.

Those photo sessions added a lot to the otherwise dull life of a dairy cow. There is a palpable depression hanging over the milking parlor already, and I understand that production is slipping. A few days ago, a couple of them tried to break out to go live at Frank Richards' farm where they could still enjoy some of the resort ambience, though they would have been chased endlessly by cutting horses. They may have to call in a bovine psychologist to deal with the situation.

The City is trying to hide their delight at the departure of the cows, but it's a pretty thin act. There were plans for "Holstein Appreciation Day," when the cows would be asked to parade down Main Street, but the fire district refused to drive their trucks through it, and you can't have a parade without the fire trucks. It got called off before it really even got put together. Mayor Brad "Buddy" Olch recently paid a visit to the Holsteins to give them a bit of a pep talk. (You didn't know that Ralph Lauren made bib overalls, did you?) He tried to assure them that their contributions to the Park City entry experience had not gone unnoticed, and that almost everybody who drives through the dairy will notice when they are gone. The City is already looking for a suitable memorial for the Holsteins, so they are not forgotten when the milking barns are knocked down and the silos are removed.

Of course, any memorial will have to be compatible with the new use of the land, which is mostly going to be to look at as we drive through it at 70 miles an hour on the new highway. There have been some discussions about building a golf course there. That would maintain the green appearance of the property, but there is nothing about the golf course that maintains the pastoral appearance of the green meadow with the black and white Holsteins grazing. Maybe if the golfers were all required to wear black and white clothes . . . . No, that would never work. These are golfers we're dealing with.

So, get your photos of the Holsteins while they are still here and feel like posing, and tonight, let's all hoist a cold glass of milk to their honor. Park City will be a different kind of place without them.

April 18, 1991

BLUE LIGHT SPECIAL

ATTENTION PARKITE SHOPPERS! There is a Blue Light Special at the new Kimball's Junction K-mart. Well, not yet, but it is before the county planning commission now, and probably will be approved. Imagine that, first a McDonalds and now a K-mart of our very own. Can Payless Shoesource be far behind? The K-mart proposal calls for a 93,000 square foot store as the anchor tenant in a 23 acre shopping center. It kind of surrounds the Chevron station at the junction. Project proponents say that we will hardly notice the K-mart store because it will be set back 1,000 feet from the road to allow for acres and acres of free, well-illuminated parking.

Ninety-three thousand square feet is a pretty big store. It's roughly twice the size of Albertsons (or about the average of the new houses in Park Meadows). And that's just one proposal. Already under construction is the Factory Stores mall. That one is supposed to be a factory outlet store, where we can all score really good deals on appropriately snooty merchandise. So far, nobody is saying who the tenants are, but a good deal is a good deal, so who cares. Pave those parking lots.

Then in addition to the two malls on either side of Highway 224, there is yet another mall planned between the

Factory Stores and Powderwood Condos, with a major, but so far unnamed, grocery store to be its anchor. And just for good measure, there is another shopping center proposed at Parkwest. That's a lot of t-shirt shops. I don't know much about the commercial real estate business, but it seems a little risky to build that much retail space to serve 4,500 people in Park City and another 5,000 in the Basin who commute to Salt Lake every day. Ours is a community of big spenders, but there are limits. Maybe they are hoping to capture the tourist dollar on the way into town. It's a little known fact that most Deer Valley skiers would stop at K-mart on their way to the slopes, if only we had a K-mart to offer.

I'm a little confused about the public reaction to all this commercial development at the junction. Personally, I thought the two gas stations were ample. When the Factory Stores mall was announced, the general reaction was pretty favorable. People seemed to think that 200,000 square feet of shopping center would be ok, as long as it had some outrageous deals on top quality merchandise. Apparently we can stand to look at a huge strip mall, if the merchandise is right. Aesthetic judgments are all relative.

But K-mart, well, that's another matter. The proposed K-mart store is receiving the Bronx cheer everywhere. Some of the opposition seems to be based on the location of the K-mart. The west side of the junction has already been spoiled with ugly signs that can be read from adjoining states. What damage can a few hundred thousand feet of strip mall do that hasn't already been done? If we get lucky, the sign on the mall will be big enough to hide the "Denny's" sign. The K-mart side of the junction is still meadow, with the exception of the Chevron that has been there since the freeway was built.

Location aside, a lot of the opposition seems to be based on K-mart itself. One Park City official was quoted on the news as saying, "We are *not* K-mart people." (K-mart is among the top three retail chains in the nation, right there with

Sears and Wal-Mart, so I suspect that some of us, in fact, *are* K-mart people.) Another said that while there is no cosmic rule that says K-mart stores have to be ugly, he has never seen one that wasn't. I get the sense that if Nordstrom proposed 93,000 square feet at the same location, the reaction might be different. We are willing to pave 23 acres of alpine meadow for 93,000 square feet of concrete block building and acres of free parking, as long as the service is good and the merchandise is up to snuff. K-mart doesn't even take American Express. They sell lawn mowers and tires right next to the lingerie. We can't have that. We have people in Park City now who have never seen the inside of a tire store.

In our relentless quest to be just like Sandy, a K-mart store is essential. How can you have a suburb without a K-mart? There are deprived children in this community who have traveled to Europe but have never been inside a K-mart store. It would be a good educational experience for them to see a K-mart store, maybe even shop there. The schools could arrange field trips to K-mart in order to broaden the horizons of the youth of our community. A trip to a Summit County K-mart would not really expose them to much. The field trip could be supplemented by a slide show featuring pictures of people from other socio-economic groups shopping at a more typical K-mart. Some of them might have to take some items out of their carts at the checkstand so they had enough money. This would have to be carefully done, however, to avoid frightening the children.

Some of the local parents might even get into the act. Nobody can resist a bargain. Of course, that presents some problems for Park City residents who would rather die than be seen at K-mart. One of the other strip malls could specialize in serving the unique needs of our community, and sell disguises to people who want to go to K-mart. For a few bucks, you could buy a special kit that equipped you for shopping at K-mart without detection. For men, there would be mustard yellow one-piece jump suits in a sturdy polyester. For the ladies, a special "hair-up-in-rollers" hat could be bought. With that kind of disguise, locals could safely shop at K-mart without being recognized. Street vendors could set up in the parking lot and sell them used Nordstrom bags to put their purchases in, just in case somebody was watching when they got home.

Apparently the planning decision has already been made to duplicate Sandy in the Snyderville Basin. Snyderville is now the biggest population center in Summit County. As long as we are going to sprawl, let's be authentic in our reconstruction of a 1970's style suburb. K-mart is an appropriate center piece for a 1970's Suburbia Theme Park. Now if we could only get a half dozen car dealerships strung out along the frontage roads . . .

[Note: When this was written, there were no car dealerships spread out along the frontage roads, and Snyderville looked even less like Sandy than it does today. Wal-Mart wasn't there. Despite predictions that it wouldn't last, K-mart and Wal-Mart have both been successful, so apparently we really are K-mart people.]

June 11, 1989

THE LADIES IN ORANGE

Most of you commuters drive out Highway 224 to Kimballs Junction, and endured your season of construction earlier this summer (and the summer before that, and the summer before that until the memory of man cannot recall when there was not construction on 224 turning that nice country road into a really ugly expressway). The first phase of that is finished, and now Salt Lake bound traffic is collecting speeding tickets where they used to collect chipped windshields.

I commute the other way, out Highway 248 to 40, and so on. That has also been under construction for a couple of years, but the new roads around the Jordanelle are on different alignments (as in the old roads will soon be under water), so there really haven't been any conflicts until just recently. Now they are tying the old roads into the new ones, and paving the new road system around the Jordanelle reservoir. Between my house and Park City I have to stop for at least five different flagperson stations, and sometimes more than that. It's getting a little old.

With that range of flag people to study, however, I have been able to learn quite a bit about flag person technique and style. I have also begun to strike up an acquaintance with some of them. At the first stop, there is a gravel truck entering the highway every ten minutes or so. This is pretty easy duty for a flag man. There are two people running this stop, a guy with a long pony tail who looks like he was left behind when the Grateful Dead left town, who does the westbound traffic, and various women who take the eastbound. None of them will take a full shift with this guy.

When the going gets slow, he cranks up the stereo in his primer gray Camaro and spends the time between truck crossings dirty dancing with his "Slow/Stop" sign on the shoulder of the road. It's kind of like American Bandstand reduced to the size of the town of Francis. He tends to get bored or hot, or both, and spins his sign around by rubbing his hands back and forth on the handle. It's a little hard to know what is happening with the sign twirling like that.

At the next stop, where the same trucks turn off the exiting road to haul gravel to a new road, there are two ladies in their 40's. One of them has a serious Diet Pepsi habit, and always has a Big Gulp the size of a wash tub plugged in with a straw. There is no privy in sight, and I don't know if she has amazing capacity, or if they get regular breaks to drive back to town. She doesn't seem too worried about traffic. She's done this for a long time, and hopes that on the next job she can get promoted to driving the detour pilot car. That's pretty easy duty, but you have to have connections with management to get that one.

Maybe because of her lack of concern, her eastbound partner takes it all pretty seriously. She doesn't just tell traffic to stop, she pleads with them. She spins her sign to "Stop" then waves, and in facial expressions that could you could lip-read from Mars, tells you to slow down, then stop. I think she used to work as a mime. She is genuinely concerned about the safety of her traffic. She wanted to be an actress, but things just didn't work out. She must be kind of new on the job; at least she has the smallest cooler. I think that is a mark of seniority. The longer they have been at it, the bigger their coolers.

Highway 40 is the most interesting part of the trip because there are days when it just isn't there. One day it will be right where it has always been. The next day there is nothing but a hole so deep that if you fell in, you could starve before you hit bottom. There are several flag people here, and they all have assistant flag people who work their way back to the end of the traffic to warn the next car to stop. There is a woman here who has really gotten into it. She started out in June kind of stiff and frightened, as well she might be, trying to stop oil tankers going 90 mph down hill with nothing more than her "Stop" sign and an orange vest for protection.

Over the summer, though, she has lightened up. The traffic doesn't bother her much. She has a new collection of different colored sun glasses, wearing the red ones one day and the green the next. She tries to match people to lost hubcaps when things are slow. My theory on her is that she raised six children alone while working as a nurse in a big city back east. When the last of the little ones left home, she packed it all in and decided to live the life of a nomadic flag lady, and see the West.

She travels from highway project to highway project, living in a VW camper. There are brief romantic encounters with equipment operators or forest rangers, but she is a gypsy at heart. When this project is finished, she's off to the next one, with no looking back. Someday, she will write a great novel about her life on the road. At least, that's my version from watching her while stuck in traffic backed up all the way to Duchesne. It's a regular soap opera, acted out right there on the shoulder of the highway.

There is another one who seems to have a training deficiency. She forgets to turn the sign around. While the sign reads "Slow" she is throwing her body in front of moving cars trying to get them to stop. Other times, the sign will be held sideways, so all you can see is the edge of it, and try to guess from the expression on her face whether you can proceed

89

safely, or are about to be run over by earth moving equipment weighing 50 tons. She also likes to test brakes and reaction time by turning the sign to "Stop" about a nano-second before the earth mover roars through the intersection. Her personal life is a mess.

It's bad enough that the flag people are taking so much of my day, but they are beginning to appear in my dreams, too. Every now and then, I will have a dream filled with sort of hard looking women wearing fluorescent orange plastic vests. One night, they all got together and sang the "Anvil Chorus" holding their "Stop/Slow" signs instead of spears, and rhythmically pounding eight-pound hammers on the lids of their plastic coolers. Other times, their signs say things besides "Slow" and "Stop." By October, we are supposed to be on the new roads, and the flag people will have moved on to other detours. Although I won't miss the inconvenience of stopping five times on the way into town, it will be kind of hard to see them go. It will be like having a whole bunch of old friends move away at once. Good luck, ladies, and watch the traffic. It's dangerous out there.

August 4, 1994

HIGHWAY 224 FINISHED
AFTER ONLY 100 YEARS

The marriage of Michael Jackson and Lisa Marie Presley is astounding. The comet smashing into Jupiter was incredible. Orrin Hatch and Ted Kennedy agreeing on Steven Bryer for the Supreme Court is unsettling. But they all seem petty compared to what we are about to witness here in Park City. It's something I never thought I would live to see: the completion of Highway 224 from Kimball's Junction to Park City. Construction on this 8 mile section of road began in 1903 when two archaeologists began excavating with teaspoons near the Parkwest turn off. Construction has proceeded at a rapid pace ever since, through several generations of Parkites. It has been UDOT's favorite project, guaranteeing lifetime employment to numerous mid-level bureaucrats.

But all of that is coming to an end. The random acts of vandalism are finally beginning to look like a highway. The contractor, and best friend of front end alignment shops everywhere, Rulon Harper, is declaring victory and going home. The road is finished. Well, almost finished. There are still some little details left to clean up, a culvert here, a stretch of pavement there, a little right of way acquisition. Still, the road is about done. Before long, UDOT will send in its crack team of rumble bar experts who will make those wide shoulders unusable for bicyclists. At the ribbon cutting, they have already selected the red neck to shoot the first hole in the "Deer Crossing" sign, and throw out the first beer can.

They are busily planting the weeds in the planters close to town. These were represented as raised, landscaped planters that were intended to distract us from the visual impact of a slab of pavement half a mile wide down the middle of the pasture. The renderings at the time showed pine trees, aspen, wildflowers and shrubs that softened the look of the road. It gave it a kind of natural, countryside look. Anybody who has been around renderings knows better, and what we have ended up with has all the charm of I-15. Pavement is pavement, and we got lots of it.

The old two lane road didn't work. There is no question that it was over capacity. When the day skiers were on the road home, it was a mess, but was bad in the off-season when the morning rush hour traffic hit the road. Of course, the physical condition of the old road didn't help things. It was poorly drained, and built up the big frost heaves in the late winter. That gave it a kind of fun-house quality, but it launched more than a few unsuspecting drivers off into the ditch.

So building a new road was a pretty logical response to the problem. I remember the shock of the community back in the Coolidge administration when the first section from the junction to Silver Springs opened for traffic. It was smooth, it was fast, but most of all, it was HUGE. There are four lane roads and then there are four lane roads with a quarter mile wide center left turn lane, two extra break-down lanes, and shoulders as wide as the Oklahoma panhandle.

People in Silver Springs discovered that the left turn to head into Park City that had been merely difficult with the old two lane road, had become absolutely impossible with the new four lane super highway. There was twice the on coming traffic to dodge, and three times the distance to cover. I drive a VW bus, and it takes me so long to get across there that I usually pack a lunch if I have to make a left turn.

92

To solve that, our pals at UDOT will install signals at a few key intersections. An article in the Salt Lake Tribune said they would be modern, computer controlled, synchronized traffic lights. Anybody who drives Foothill Drive in Salt Lake at rush hour knows how well *that* works. So in a relatively short time, we will have reproduced the jammed traffic and gridlock condition that existed before all of this started. That will push the flow of traffic out to 248, which is a narrow, two lane road kind of like 224 used to be. Progress is a wonderful thing.

The completion of the road is an important event for Park City. For the first time in generations, Harper Construction won't have broken down machinery littering the road like a scene from the Iraqi evacuation of Kuwait. The flaggers will be retired to the flagger hall of fame. Some of them started as teenagers, and will now retire. To commemorate this great period in Park City's history, I suggest that we commission a bronze monument to the Unknown Flagger to install in one of the planters in the middle of the road.

The statue would show a woman flagger in tight jeans and her orange vest, one foot resting on top of her cooler, Big Gulp and Marlboro in hand. She would be giving that "slow down" wave, with her "stop" sign leaning on her shoulder. The sun would shimmer on the polished surface of her hard hat.

The statue would be executed on a heroic scale, maybe ten feet high, to remind all who pass by that long before there were trust funders, or pilots, or realtors, or skiers, or even miners in Park City, there were thousands of flaggers stopping traffic for unexplained reasons for long periods of time. They are an important part of our history, and with the completion of the road, they will fade into memory.

Of course no new highway is complete until they dig the first hole in it. After a decade of moving utilities around, I'm sure there is something that is in the wrong place, too small, or worn out since this project started. So I have a little pool going with some friends on when the first excavation in the new road will take place. The winner has to pick the date, the utility company, and the location to win. I've got Mountain Fuel, the first week in October, at Ridgeview Drive. A friend thinks I'm all wrong, and has picked Snyderville Basin Sewer District, within ten minutes of the ribbon cutting, at the Holiday Ranch intersection.

My house is on a one lane dirt road. The traffic in the neighborhood has increased to a point that we no longer have a strip of grass down the middle of the road. A year ago, there was some discussion about paving it, but the majority of the people said no, they would prefer to pull out the culverts and roughen it up a little. New roads attract traffic the way horses attract flies.

We've really done it now in Park City, with a freeway running right into Albertsons. We can double the flow of traffic into town. But there's still no place to park.

August 20, 1992

HOUSE PAINTING THOUGHTS

The last few evenings, I've been working at painting the window and door frames on my house. It is a job that should have been done last fall, and wasn't, and so it is harder this year. There's more scraping, sanding and priming than would have been needed if I had been on top of things last year. It's a slow process, since I fit it in around everything else, and only want the windows out of the house one or two at a time. An assembly line process would be more efficient, but the rain would blow in.

Standing out in the driveway, with the window sash on a sawhorse, I end up taking a longer view of the neighborhood. Mine is not exactly a bustling place. Three or four cars might go down the lane all day--a few more on weekends. Change is slow here. Much of the surrounding land is owned by the families who owned it at the turn of the last century, and will still own it at the turn of the next one. My own family is into its fourth generation here, if a couple of new-born babies get counted.

So in the late afternoon-into-evening, slapping paint and listening to the river roll by, all kinds of thoughts wandered through. The man who first installed the water line that has more or less consumed my summer turned 100 this year. He was younger than me when he installed the pipe from the spring to the dairy barn. He's still around, and when he heard that we were upgrading the line, his only comment was, "That spring is a real dandy."

Another painting session was briefly interrupted by visitors. My mother was having a party for some friends she has known since college. That's reaching back a few years. Of the eight couples, there are now three widows. There are nearly 400 years of marriage represented among her dinner guests. They walked across the bridge from her house to the path along the river, and stopped to comment on my color selection. I don't think any of them liked it. I was afraid it was too conservative, but I guess not.

I could have hired the painting done, and probably get both a better and quicker job. Professional painters can slide over things that are taking me a long time to work around. I'm not sure they would need to bother with masking tape. That alone takes about as long as the painting. But I like painting my own house, and making the seasonal repairs around the place. The brush strokes and squashed bugs from my last paint job are still evident.

When I was about five or six, my cousin and I built a "fort" out of old cinder blocks and logs. The fort was just about where my garage sits now. Somehow, when there is no intention of selling a house, going over it with the kind of careful examination that painting the trim requires is ok. I know where the siding is warping, and what the woodpeckers have done.

Another evening, standing there in the driveway, I saw the neighborhood change forever. A van with the name of a Salt Lake mortuary arrived at the intersection of the lane going up-stream from the highway. The people in that area have been here for a hundred years. I haven't had much occasion to get acquainted with most of them, the 60 year difference in ages and locked gates on both their lane and ours has relegated the relationship to one of brief hellos at the cluster of mail boxes, theirs on one side of the highway and ours on the other.

Mrs. Romney, one of the older members of that family had died quietly, alone in a cabin her parents had built before World War I. She had entertained a large crowd of family and friends the evening before. Watching the van from the mortuary turn in the upstream lane brought back memories of last summer when the same van was calling at my father's house, which had a lot to do with why the windows didn't get painted last year.

The new owner of another house on the downstream lane, past mine, arrived and took possession. The deal had been in escrow for months and finally closed. He is a nice guy, somebody I have met a couple of times in the course of his purchase of the house. We hiked around to find the survey corners, and I showed him where the water line cuts through his lot without benefit of an easement.

We stood in my driveway, leaning against cars and talking about the usual new-neighbor stuff like when the garbage truck comes and where to put it. I noticed his car still has California plates. He would never have met our late neighbor at the mailboxes, and probably didn't understand the significance of the dark blue van he passed on the bridge. There was certainly no point in telling him.

He is moving into a tiny cabin. The house has never been used as anything other than a weekend getaway before, and he may freeze this winter. The blue van could be back. I've always been the only permanent resident on this lane. Now there are two. Talk about exploding populations-- doubled over night. He works in the city, and will have to leave early to get to work on time. Most of the summer, I wake to the sound of the sand hill cranes moving from their nesting grounds to the hay fields where they spend the day. Now I will probably wake to the sound of tires crunching gravel on an early morning commute.

Arrangements will have to be made about plowing the snow. There was never been any reason to plow beyond my house before. Another mail box will crop up at the shoulder of the road, and on Tuesdays, there will be a bigger pile of garbage out there waiting to be picked up. Another UPS customer whose packages get left at my cousin's house because it is right on the main road and she is usually home during the day.

By twilight, it's time to stick the brush in the thinner to soak until tomorrow's session. The moon comes up over the ridge, and I hear a couple of cows bellowing at each other in the pasture across the river. The normal patterns of evening go on unchanged. But everything is different. One neighbor quietly slips away forever, and another arrives, enthusiastically talking about remodeling, adding on, getting involved. Change is as certain as the sunrise.

There are still four more windows and the frames on the second floor to do. I wonder if I can get one gallon of paint to stretch that far.

November 5, 1992

NEW PHONE BOOK TELLS IT ALL

I've certainly read better books. The plot line is pretty thin, and while it's full of characters, there isn't much information about any of them. I'm not talking about the latest Stephen King thriller. This is a review of the Heber City/Park City phone book for 1992-93. A review of the phone book? You've got to be kidding! Nope. Every now and then, if you want to take the pulse of a community, read the phone book. It's as good as the census, but it comes out every year.

Just by coincidence of sloppy housekeeping, I happen to have phone books from the past three years around the house. The 1990 phone book (which has been propping up a book case with a short leg) stands out as a favorite of mine because it is the first time in years that Kamas, which is served by a little independent phone company, was included in the US West phone book. It was like tearing down the Berlin Wall. Of course the map in the front material showing how to call from one area to another, and which calls are long distance, still doesn't show the Kamas Valley as anything but a big empty space, but that's ok. The zoning map should be so clear.

Anyway, in October of 1990, the Park City portion of the phone book, the white pages, was 49 pages long, with only about a quarter page on the last one. The current phone book has 58 pages of Park City listings, an increase of 9 pages or

18% over two years. There were 54 pages in the in-between year.

More surprising to me is the addition of new prefixes. When I moved to Park City, nobody ever gave a 7 digit phone number. Everybody was 649, so only the last four mattered. Then there was the 645 prefix, and that caused no end of confusion because Heber City is 654, and the similarity was more than some of us could easily adapt to. That's when I packed up and moved to Woodland. We only had one prefix, and on local calls, you didn't even have to dial it.

For the 1992 phone book, Park City has a whole slug of prefixes. There is 649, 645, and just when we were getting used to that, they spring 647 on us. The realtors and others in the mobile phone elite can be reached on 640 (but those who call generate a lot of extra radio waves that may be destroying the planet, so it better be important). The phone book also shows a 659 prefix for Park City. I don't know what that is, and when I tried to call the phone company to find out, all I got was a busy signal.

Kamas has seen its listings expand from 10 pages in 1990 to 12 pages in 1992. Heber has gone from 26 to 29, and Coalville from 8 to 9 pages. It looks like Kamas is bigger than Coalville these days.

The white pages listings are a general indicator of population growth, but it doesn't really say much about the nature of the town. If you really want to know the mood of a place, read the Yellow Pages. For example, in 1990, there were 29 lawyers listed in the Yellow Pages for Park City. The vast majority of them were located in Salt Lake and ran local ads so the venerable senior partner could deduct his Park City condo as a business expense. This year, without a real surge in condo sales, there are 44 lawyers listed, and better than half of them have a local address. I'm not sure what it says about a community when the number of lawyers nearly doubles in just 2 years, but it can't be entirely good news.

A little random checking reveals that Park City has more sushi bars than gas stations, more places to buy furs than tires, and not a single funeral home. There are listings for 9 massage therapists. There are no massage therapists in Kamas, Heber, or Coalville, though each of those towns has both a funeral home and a meat packing plant. There were only 3 massage therapists in the 1990 yellow pages for Park City. Is there any correlation between the sudden growth in people seeking the relaxation and stress relief of a massage and the doubling of the number of lawyers?

Just for comparison, in Salt Lake's Yellow Pages, serving a population of half a million, there are 43 massage places listed, and not all of them look like legitimate therapists. That's about one rubbor for nearly 12,000 rubbees. In the Park City area, with a population of about 10,000, we have 9, or about one massage therapist for every 1,000 people.

Meanwhile, the number of locally based plumbers dropped. The thickness of the Yellow Pages devoted to backed up drains has actually grown, but most of the listings now are for Salt Lake based plumbers who are willing to drive up the canyon for the right price. The number of real live, local, get 'em on Sunday night plumbers in Park City has shrunk. They all went to law school (though the money is better in plumbing).

Our phone book is still the small format phone book. I don't know how thick it has to get before they start printing in on the larger paper like the Salt Lake directory. We can probably grow a while before having to re-arrange the desk drawer to hold the bigger phone book.

One of the most annoying things about this year's phone book is the inclusion of a stiff card between the white and Yellow Pages to separate them in case you can't tell the difference between the colored paper. This card is, of course, advertising space. It is good advertising, too, since the first thing I noticed flipping through the new phone book was this stiff card in the middle that made it impossible to keep the book open to the page I wanted. I got a paper cut that nearly took my thumb off.

But that's when I noticed the significance of the now blood smeared ad. This stiff sheet in the middle of the phone book has ads for lawyers on both sides of it. Personal injuries on one side, and drunk driving on the other. I looked to see if there was a listing for lawyers specializing in cases involving the loss of thumbs resulting from paper cuts received from annoying, stiff cardboard sheets in the middle of the phone book with pictures of lawyers on them. There weren't any, but the high priced ad got torn out of my phone book the first time I had to look up a number.

One of the classic bits of phone book lore was told to me by Rick Brough. He opened the local phone book to the map pages, with Heber City's streets laid out in its nice grid pattern, and Park City's looking like a plate of spaghetti that got spilled. "This is your town," he said pointing to Heber. He moved his pointer to the Park City page and said, "This is your town on drugs."

The 1989 book was the first year that Kamas was in the same phone book as the rest of Summit County. I knew something was up when I got a copy of the "Heber City/Park City" phone book at home, over in Woodland. It was right there in my mailbox. Big deal, you say? Well, it is. The Greater Kamas Metroplex, comprised of Oakley, Peoa, Marion, Samak, Kamas, Francis and Woodland are all served by the Kamas-Woodland Telephone Company, a division of Consolidated Kite-String Communications. It is a small but sincere utility with the latest equipment. We now have to dial all seven numbers to place a call. The rest of Summit and Wasatch Counties, and most of Utah, are served by US West Communications. They used to be Mountain Bell until they changed the name a year ago to make things more confusing.

Until 1989 all of the rest of Summit and Wasatch Counties were all neatly published in a single phone book, those of us in the Kamas area were left out. The area served by Kamas-Woodland Telephone was not even shown on the maps in the front of the phone book. It was just a big empty spot, kind of like China used to be on State Department maps.

Oh, sure, we had our own phone book, with a pretty country scene with horses or mountains on the cover. It had all the local listings in it, and also complete listings for the rest of Summit and Wasatch Counties. We were reaching out, hoping to open communications with the rest of the area. Mountain Bell wouldn't let us in their phone book. The Kamas book was mailed to every box holder in Park City each year, and judging by the pile of them by the trash cans in the Post Office, probably not one in a hundred made it out the door. It sent the message that you didn't want to talk to us. I've heard your conversations on the street: "Anything in the mail today?"

"Nope. Just a funny little phone book from Kamas. I threw it away."

"Good. There's nobody over there we need to call."

But as of 1989, eight-and-a-half pages worth of Kamas numbers are there for your convenience. Where else can you find listings for a whole column's worth of Woolstenhulmes? Certainly not in the Park City listings, there isn't even one.

Uniting our telephone listings is kind of a trivial thing in a lot of ways, but I really think it is the beginning of something better. Maybe it marks the beginning of a united Summit and Wasatch County. If the phone companies recognize the communities in these two counties are a single economic unit for purposes of publishing the yellow pages, maybe even the local governments can see that full diplomatic relations would be a good thing for the economic future of the whole area.

I do miss the picture of the horses on the cover, though.

November 9, 1995

SOCIAL EVENT OF THE SEASON

I can go for years and years without going to a grand opening at a grocery store, but I've managed to hit two in the last few months. First the new Foodtown opened in Kamas, and now Dan's is open in Park City. The pre-opening party at Dan's may have been the social event of the season. Or maybe I need to get out more . . . Anyway, it was quite a party.

The store wasn't open. There were politely worded signs posted reminding people that even though they were in a fully stocked grocery store, they couldn't buy anything that night. The aisles were loaded in ways that they probably won't be again. Every bottle of spaghetti sauce had its label lined up with the bottle below, and faced the aisle perfectly. Because nothing was for sale, there were no places where things had been taken off the shelf. Nobody had stuck a jar of mayonnaise they didn't want on the shelf next to the canned beans. It looked too perfect. The produce was stacked up like a still life photo shoot. There was a full spread of food laid out at what looks a lot like a great new restaurant, but it was all for show. With no carts in the aisles, people were walking around socializing. There were no screaming kids dumping coffee beans on the floor or crushing the bread.

Hostesses in formal uniforms wandered up and down the paper goods and frozen food aisles passing out samples of brownies, smoked salmon, and other treats. Local residents wandered around trying to make a meal of it. A happy looking couple sang folk songs in the check stands. There was something surreal about a pretty high-brow party in the grocery store. People were wearing suits and dresses, looking like June and Ward Cleaver going to the A & P, or a party at the Country Club. In one corner, there is a new bank--West Washington Interstate Security One First--or something like that. Park City now has a different bank for every day of the week but Sunday.

It's been a long time since Park City had two grocery stores. The last time was when Alpha-Beta (now Albertson's) opened up. The Mount Air Market managed to hang on for a while, but in a town less than half the size we are now--and Snyderville didn't exist at all--the little local store couldn't stand up to a national giant. Over the years, we have outgrown our one-market status. I think even the Albertson's people were ready to have another store in town.

There were lots of people at the Dan's Grand Opening party I didn't know. Some were employees, others were contractors, vendors, equipment suppliers, or wholesalers. The place was pretty packed. There were also some locals there, including politicians who were chasing people up and down the aisles. That will reverse after the election, and the elected officials will be the ones on the run. At one point the crowd stampeded out of the cake mix and baking supplies aisle. I was afraid there had been a gas leak or something. But it was just one of our intrepid candidates causing the citizenry to flee. They had heard all they wanted to from him already.

I got trapped by a couple of politicians, who were willing to take full credit for this wonderful new store. In fact, I think it was an idea of one of the candidates that the new Dan's store should have shopping carts with round wheels that work. "That was a condition of approval. Boy are we tough on these

106

developers." Yep, the whole thing happened because of the Process.

That's not exactly how I remember one of the most drawn out reviews in history, and the store is opening about a year later than planned. The Gardiner family, who have signed the loans to build and stock the place probably would like to think they deserve some small measure of the credit for building the new store. But a day or two ahead of the election, politicians can take credit for about anything. One candidate is personally responsible for the sunrise.

The store is pretty amazing. There is ostrich meat for $19.99 a pound, and buffalo at something close to it. They also have Hamburger Helper. The beverage buyer was apparently instructed to stock as many obscure beer labels as possible. There is a whole aisle of beer, and I'd guess over 50 brands from Old Milwaukee to designer label, wooden crated, souvenir six packs of Wasatch. The bakery looks like the dessert selection at Deer Valley. I'm not a big vegetable eater, and can be pretty easily satisfied with a bag of frozen peas and carrots, but the produce section has exotic stuff there I didn't even recognize.

The most amazing thing to me, though, was that they had ripe bananas for sale. Ever since Alpha Beta sold out to the other guys, bananas have been sold green and hard enough to drive nails with. If you want a banana today, you'd better have bought it a month ago. Now you can get ripe bananas at Dan's.

The store opened for real on Monday, and I was there with a lot of other curious locals stocking up. The shopping carts actually do have 4 functioning wheels on each one. People were back with their kids running amok in the store, throwing tantrums in the aisles, just like a regular market. People were doing a sort of inspection, and comparing things mentally to what they were used to. "How many different brands of tissue does the other place offer?" "I wonder what I've been paying for this across the street." Price comparison was never really an option before. Of course, Park City being what it now is, the only price comparison that is likely to matter is the upper end, allowing a gushing hostess to announce that the ostrich meat was $20 a pound, but she used to have to fly it in at twice that. This is not a big Jell-O or macaroni and cheese town.

Having a second grocery store in town will cut the time spent in the check out lines a lot. But the big change is that it will wreck havoc on our whole political system. It's been possible to go to Albertson's and, in the course of a single shopping trip, run into several council members, planning commissioners, school board members or officials. Any citizen with a minor grievance or complaint could be assured of finding some official ear at the grocery store. It was the marketplace in the ancient Greek model, where everybody went. It was the common denominator of town.

Now, with two grocery stores, there is the potential for a split, with the local politics dividing into Dan's shoppers and Albertson's shoppers. The whole political dynamic will change when you can't count on finding an elected officials every time you hit the store, or only certain people will be at your store of choice, while others hang out at the "other" store. Shopping for politicians will be a lot more complicated than in the old days when you could find them among the other fruits and vegetables. During future campaigns, candidates will have to double their grocery shopping exposure. Things will never be the same again.

October 12, 1995

TEARING 'EM DOWN:
SECOND GROWTH HOUSING

A couple of years ago, a classic book about life in a resort town came out. It was *White-out: Lost in Aspen*, by Ted Connover. It ought to be required reading for anybody moving into a resort town. Realtors should be required to give copies of it to their victims--er, customers--along with copies of the subdivision covenants. People might actually read the book. Nobody ever reads the covenants until the lawsuits start flying.

One of the chapters in *White-out* that sticks with me described his invitation to an open house of the real estate kind, where local realtors were feted with wine and cheese at the first showing of a prestige property. It was one of those huge homes with thousands of square feet of space filled with thousands of dollars of furnishings. Connover was living in some cramped apartment that probably had olive green shag carpet and boomerang pattern Formica counter tops. To him, the house was a palace. Everybody at the party was commenting on the view, but nobody said much about the house, the quality woodwork, the rock fireplace, or the obviously high level of finish and overall quality construction.

As the evening wore on, he finally figured it out. The house was only about ten years old, but the house wasn't really on the market. The *lot* was on the market. The house, all upper six figures' worth of it, was a tear-down. The likely purchaser of the property was after the location alone, and would scrape off the nearly new luxury home to build something more spacious, more luxurious, more tasteful, and above all else, *more*.

Reading that chapter, I tried to calm myself by leaning back on my couch (purchased from Sears on the installment plan) and thinking that Park City would never come to that. Park City is already fairly well along on the weirdness scale compared to real towns where people have jobs and more or less mind their own business. But, if there is a good side to our proximity to Salt Lake, it was an occasional dose of sanity from regular people. Park City would never hit the point of tearing down almost new, luxurious housing, just to build something more garishly consumptive on the site. It could never happen here.

I was wrong. The City has issued a demolition permit for a house in American Flag. This is not a remodel. Apparently the house on the lot was so bad that adding on and covering up was not enough. This is a demolition permit-- scrape it down to bare earth, nothing left but the sewer pipe (which is probably in the wrong location) and start over. That's an interesting twist on the growth control theme--second growth housing.

American Flag has been one of the high-tone neighborhoods in Park City since it was platted about ten years ago. It's the home of Johnny Carson and others of his ilk. The annual property taxes on a place in American Flag would buy a Homestake condo. We are not talking about blight. This is not some double-wide with old tires on the roof and engine blocks in the front yard. It's hard to imagine anything in Deer Valley deserving of being torn down.

Well, there is that place that looks like a branch bank. It's a pretty attractive branch bank, the kind you would see in an expensive suburb of Los Angeles. But it still looks more like a bank than a house. You see it from the ski run, and Deer Valley skiers are always commenting on how convenient it is to have a

110

ski-in, ski-out bank available. I understand people are always knocking on the door asking to cash checks or looking for the ATM machine.

That's not the one. I saw an ad for that one in the paper for something over $4 million (deposits insured to $100,000 by the FDIC). The bank will stay. So some other perfectly good house in a neighborhood of $3 to $4 million dollar houses is about to get the wrecking ball.

At first, the idea of tearing down a house that has to be better than what 95% of the American people will ever live in, just to build a house that is better than 98% of the American people's houses is disgusting. It seems so wasteful of craftsmanship, materials, and cash.

But after giving it some thought, maybe this is the solution to our local desire to have growth and limit it at the same time. If we harvest housing the way they harvest trees in the northwest, maybe we can treat growth as a renewable resource. For example, without paving another inch of road, annexing more land, or platting a new subdivision, our growth-based economy can keep right on functioning.

With a tear down, architects, engineers, and all the building trades get to reap the benefits of building another house, without increasing the size of town, or the potential population increase that would result from building a new house on a virgin lot. The City should be happy, since the planners get to meddle in the design of somebody else's house, stake new limits of disturbance, and otherwise fill their time with something other than the Flagstaff Annexation. They keep busy. A new round of impact, plan check, permit, and other fees will be collected. Realtors will get a second round of commissions.

So in the end, there is a tremendous stirring of economic activity from the demolition of the $2 million house to replace it with the $5 million house, but no net increase in the number of houses in town. It makes sense in that warped American way of doing things. We ought to look at clear-cutting other

111

neighborhoods to start over. Now if I could just figure out which land fill the old mansion will be dumped in, I can probably fix my place up a little.

February 14, 1998

LES METERS DU PARQUING ALA FRANCAIS

If you didn't blow off work and spend last week skiing, you probably need to reconsider why you are living here. After what has been a pretty disappointing winter season, it got good last week, starting with a deep powder Sunday. It was snowing hard enough to fill in your tracks behind you, so every run was essentially untracked powder. It did wonders for the overall attitude. And, as things go, the general attitude around town is much in need of improvement. The tourist traffic is staying home this year. They are probably busy sand-bagging their houses in rain-soaked California. Those who aren't flooding are probably taking vacations someplace where it isn't likely to storm. They've had enough.

So business is down. The resorts aren't selling as many lift tickets as usual. Deer Valley has even been selling discounted tickets through Smith's grocery stores, trying to drum up a little more local traffic. People in the lodging business aren't grumbling out loud, but nobody is all that happy. And the retailers on Main Street are in a snit because they are getting the double whammy of lower than normal tourist traffic and locals staying away because of the new parking meters. The City Council has responded by saying that they might make paid parking a year-round deal, just to avoid having to listen to all the bellyaching again next fall. It's a perfect marketing approach to a perfect program. Shut-up and take your medicine.

But up skiing the other day, in conditions so perfect that nothing else really mattered, it occurred to me that the unpleasantness is mostly an issue of attitude. This parking deal just wasn't marketed properly. Some people look at the system that is confusing, inconvenient, urban, and annoying and see only that it is confusing, inconvenient, urban and annoying. Others look at it, and conclude that a neutron bomb went off on Main Street and they can park anywhere they want. Under the influence of too many powder turns on a perfect day, I came to realize that with a little different spin, there were better ways of looking at the parking system. With a little imagination, it can almost be fun.

For example, I like to travel, but haven't been much farther than Coalville for quite a while. But now, when I go to Main Street, with just a little imagination, I feel like I'm in a foreign country. I'm instantly transported to a place where I don't know the language or customs of the people. The simplest devices confound and amaze. There is a real sense of adventure in dealing with *les meters du parquing ala Francais.* In Salt Lake or other regular American places, the parking meters are simple, and more or less alike. Here in Park City, we have to deal with the twisted workings of the French mind that would design such a system. These are the same people who manufacture the Citroen. It feels quite exotic. The public relations campaign could have picked up on that aspect. "Travel the world by parking on Main Street."

The merchants are trying to overcome the resistance to the meters by passing out tokens. The City mailed "smart cards" to a select list. They used the water department billing list, which means that anybody living in an apartment didn't get their free parking smart card. Kind of selected the wrong end of the economic ladder there, didn't they? It was all very well thought out.

114

There are also some free-lance token pushers out there. A friend told me about an incident just the other night, in that dark, echo-filled tunnel next to the Egyptian Theater. She was approached by a seedy looking guy who stepped out of the shadows. He offered her a token. "No," she said, "I don't do tokens."

"How do you know what you're turning down if you don't try it?" he said. "It feels real good having a parking place out there. Real good. Tell you what. How about I give you your first token for free, just so you can try it and decide for yourself if you like it or not?" His tone was a little threatening

"I really don't think so," she said. Where is a cop when you want one?

"I've got tokens, smart cards, hang tags. Anything you like. Just give it a try. I'll be your parking connection."

My friend finally accepted a token just to get the guy to leave her alone and get out of the tunnel. She fed the illicit token to a meter. Later she told me, "I couldn't enjoy my dinner because I was already wondering where my next token was going to come from."

Les meters du parquing ala Francais are technological marvels. To make it easier, the system has the hang tags you can conveniently buy next time you are in the Public Works Garage inspecting the snow plows. With the hang tags, which are sold mostly to locals, you have a couple of options for making the parking system more interesting. You can pretend to be a character in a Tom Clancy novel, and that your hang tag is really a car bomb set to explode in a crowed (or in this case, a vacant) marketplace in (choose your own plot) Belfast, Jerusalem, Nagano, or wherever. You park your car, look around to see if you've been observed, and then set the timer to blow the car and everything around it to smithereens while you are sipping cappuccino at some trendy restaurant. On the way back from dinner, you can switch to a different plot line, and

115

you are now the hero, rushing back to the car to diffuse the bomb just in the nick of time. You rescue Sandra Bullock, and drive her home so she doesn't have to get on the bus.

The other big appeal of the hang tag is that it helps differentiate between locals and visitors. It's a little bit of technology you can hang in the window that says "I'm a local and you're not." I've never fully understood the appeal of that, but there's no question that it is part of the social underpinning of the town. It's like having a 649 phone number or a three digit post office box at the main post office. The city will probably sell a hang tag to somebody who lives in the 84098 ZIP code and has a 658 phone number, but I think they would have better market acceptance if there was some sense of exclusivity to the hang tags. If just anybody can get one, nobody wants one.

There's no doubt about it, the parking meters have freed up lots of parking on Main Street and Swede Alley. And I suspect that once you figure out how to work the meters, or buy your hang tag (I still haven't done either) the system ought to work. Maybe they ought to teach it in the schools, or install training meters in the grocery stores, where people can learn how to work them in a private booth, rather than standing out there in the snow, looking like an idiot trying to figure them out. From the people I've talked to, it's not the 50 cents that is the problem. It's learning how to work them, and the embarrassment factor in not being able to work a parking meter while your out-of-town guests are standing there thinking "What kind of idiot can't work a parking meter? We've got to get these people back to the city for their own good. Their brains have turned to mush up here in the thin air."

ATM machines had the same kind of resistance at the beginning. We all learned to use them, and would revolution would break out if those were suddenly taken out. I suspect even the most Luddite of us (like me) can be taught how to use

116

les meters du parquing ala Francais. But for the time being, business is brisk at Prospector area restaurants.

April 4, 1998

SO LONG TO THE COOKIE BEAR

On Wednesday, I was going up skiing. I stopped at the Cookie Bear for my usual pre-ski energizer of two chocolate chip cookies with walnuts and a Coke. I walked in, and there was the store owner, Jana Cole, boxing up the last of the bears. The cookies were already gone. The Cookie Bear is closed. As Monty Python said about the parrot, "gone, deceased, ceased to be." I've followed the resort base area expansion as it has ground through the planning process. It will probably take less time to build the building that it did to get the permit, which I think is some kind of badge of honor among government planners. The old gondola building is coming down, and in its place is a new time share project. I've even been involved in the process a little from time to time. So the closing of the Cookie Bear wasn't news. The gondola was taken out last year in preparation for the wrecking ball.

But it was a real shock to walk in there and find Jana boxing up the last of the critters. There is a difference between knowing that the building is being torn down, and actually being denied chocolate chip cookies because of it. There were guys walking around the outside of the building wearing tool belts, carrying tape measures and pointing to parts of the building that might be especially vulnerable to the wrecking ball. The demolition crew was on deck. *Run, Jana, run! Get*

119

out while you still can! Steeps, the little sundry and souvenir store, the ski storage place, and the seasonal lockers are also closing up. Gart Brothers has apparently decided to stay until their lease runs out, and I guess they will tear the building down around them.

The Cookie Bear has been in business for about 15 years, and the last 10 of that have been at the corner adjacent to the ticket window. That's the designated meeting place to hook up with friends for a day of skiing. "9:30 at the Bear," is all the message anybody has had to leave on the answering machine. The "earlier if it snows" is implicit. Most times, we don't even need that much of a message. It's just understood. I'm not sure how to go skiing without the Cookie Bear as the first stop. Maybe that's why I don't ski Deer Valley very often. We spend half the morning looking for each other.

It was close to the lifts, close to the ticket window so anybody without a pass was already right there. But it was more than a convenient meeting place. Parking in the lower lot and going up Eagle is a lot more convenient way to get on the mountain, but waiting for the group to assemble at the Bear was better. There was a cup of coffee and a muffin for some, and a Coke and a couple of cookies for those of us with a serious sweet tooth problem. Jana, or more often, Jana's Mom would be baking the cookies for the morning rush. Jana's Mom isn't as famous as Dave Letterman's Mom, but close. The other employees were part of the morning ritual. As a regular, they would sometimes slip me a hot cookie right out of the oven, and knew they didn't need to warn me about burning my tongue on the melted chocolate. The phone was available to find out if there had been last minute changes in plans. Cookie Bear was the mountain concierge. We left messages with them for late arrivals. All for the price of a couple of cookies.

I seldom ended the day there, but there has been a generation of Park City kids who have finished their ski day at the Cookie Bear. I think they start the day with "If you work really hard in your ski lesson, and don't whine, we can get cookies when we're done." Everybody has their own apres ski reward, and for the under 12 crowd, it has been the Cookie Bear.

The resort plaza has seen a lot of changes through the years. I haven't really kept track, but my memory is that back in 1963, when I started skiing Park City (boy does that make me sound old), the parking lot extended right up to the steps of the Gondola building, and the ticket office was sort of where the Cookie Bear is/was. The ski school took us up Payday, and lunch was a hot dog in the cafeteria that later became Steeps. Marsac Mill Manor and the Silver Mill House condos weren't there, and the Victorian facade hadn't been stuck over the 1960's "pseudo-European ski area vernacular" architecture of the gondola building. That was it at the base. And the resort base felt like it was a million miles away from downtown Park City.

What is now the Sweetwater condo project was the *C'est Bon* Lodge, complete with a Polynesian theme restaurant. Don't ask me why there were grass shack restaurant booths in a ski area. They had the world's greasiest fried shrimp. There was a scandalous stripper named Shirley who danced there on Friday and Saturday nights, and the posters advertising her show were all over the place. By the time I was old enough to get into the show, Shirley was old enough that she kept her clothes on. Grass shack restaurant décor went out of fashion, and, in the ultimate collapse, it became a timeshare project at a time when timeshare projects were regarded as one notch below strippers and greasy shrimp among polite company. The Silver King Hotel (the first, cinder-block Motel-6 looking version, not what's there now) was the up-scale lodging in town at the time. The Miner's Hospital stood where Shadow Ridge Hotel is now. It operated as a flop house, with cheap rooms that housed some of the town's respectable in their ski bum days.

Later the first condos popped up. I remember pretty clearly parking the car (I was driving myself up skiing then) walking up between the two new buildings, and wondering if I could find the ticket window. Later still came the new ticket office building, the resort center condos and that dark underground garage.

Wednesday, I left the cookie-less Cookie Bear after signing a big card for Jana and wishing her well. I took the new high speed Payday and Bonanza lifts up the line of the old gondola. There was a time in my life that the only reason I was willing to go skiing at all was that I thought riding up the gondola was the coolest thing this side of Disneyland. I took a few runs on Silverlode, which will always be Prospector to me. I took one run down the line of the old Lost Prospector double chair, remembering the terrible lift lines that built up, even with two side by side double chairs. I had a Coke at the Summit House, the architectural twin to the gondola building, and watched a bunch of kids squirting ketchup all over creation the way I did years ago. That building hasn't changed much through the years. Sometimes a good fire is not such a bad idea. I remember it with flags hanging from the rafters. But instead of flags of foreign countries, they were flags of different departments at the resort: "Lifts" "Transportation" "Maintenance" "Food Service" and stuff like that. There wasn't much that attracted national attention here then.

I took a couple more runs, but the light was flat and the wind was howling, and I hadn't had any cookies that morning to start the day off right.

By the start of next season, the old gondola building will be a great big hole in the ground (maybe with Gart Brothers floating in the middle of it). The new buildings will house new businesses, and new traditions will work themselves out. My friends and I will find some place other than the

Cookie Bear to meet in the morning. Who knows, we might even meet someplace and car pool over to the hill. The new lifts have really made the mountain more accessible, and skiing on Payday is even kind of fun without that long lift ride on the old triple chair. But I sure do miss those cookies.

October 17, 1998

PARK CITY'S NEW AUTO DEALERSHIP

The thing I like best about Park City is that, just when I think it can't get any more absurd, it does. There is nothing unusual about a town this size being without a car dealership. There is nothing all that unusual about a town this size having only one car dealership. Park City survived for years with only Mawhinney Motors on Park Avenue, until the City bought the building and the Chevy dealer moved out to the Snyderville Auto Mall. But there is something really over the top about a town whose only car dealership is a Ferrari agency. For years now, I've driven a clunky Toyota pickup. It's reliable, it gets me where I need to go, it's good in the snow, and it's boring as a County Planning Commission meeting. Now you can buy a Ferrari without leaving town. Finally, our long nightmare is over.

I was invited to the grand opening of Landshark Racing's new Ferrari dealership across from the Lost Sock Laundromat. Technically, it's not a new dealership. They have just relocated their business from Salt Lake to Park City. It's mostly a used car dealership, for those looking to spend $250,000 on a previously owned car. But still, if we are only going to have one car dealer in town, it might as well be a Ferrari dealer.

The grand opening was quite the affair. Several public officials were there, local racing enthusiasts, and a lot of friends. I normally don't go to the grand openings of car dealerships. I don't think I was invited to the opening of the Chevrolet dealership out in Snyderville. If I was, I didn't go. Chevrolet. I-80 frontage road. Hotdogs. I don't think so. But the opening of the Ferrari dealership was an event. Nobody was giving away ballpark hotdogs or balloons for the kids.

125

This was upscale. I didn't recognize a single item on the hors d'oeuvre platter.

The dealership is a nice little show room, with great murals of Italian street scenes on the walls. There is a picture of Enzo Ferrari looking out the window at one end of the mural, and a woman who I'm quire sure wasn't Mrs. Ferrari at another window. I think she was an intern. There were four cars on the lot ranging in price from $238,000 to a sort of embarrassing old Porsche for a mere $58,000. I tried to work a deal involving my '55 Studebaker truck as a trade, and was politely ushered out.

Like a lot of people in Park City, I moved here in a Volkswagen bus. I started working in Park City and commuted up the canyon from Salt Lake in the VW. It was an icebox on wheels. I learned to drive it wearing a sleeping bag. It was a great pleasure to actually move to town so I could walk to work in sub-zero temperatures rather than drive in the unheated Volkswagen. But Volkswagens were the car of choice in Park City at the time. The top of the line was the Squareback sedan, that little station wagon looking model. The Squarebacks had the advantage of being big enough to hold your skis and dogs, but small enough that the pathetic VW heaters of the day could actually clear a tiny porthole in the frost on the windshield. The bigger volume of the bus made it impossible to detect any heat at all. Bus or Squareback, they were good in the snow, cheap, started in the cold, and got good gas mileage.

The social history of Park City could almost be told by motor vehicle registrations. As my wave of newcomers started to get a little money ahead, people decided that they could upgrade their cars. Usually the birth of a child dictated getting a car with a heater in it, and the old VWs started being replaced with Saabs on the upper end, Subarus for the masses, VWs for the single. The Sport Ubiquitous Vehicle hadn't been invented yet, except for a few eccentrics like the International Scout. People in the building trades could get away with driving full sized Ford pickups with four wheel drive, but the gas mileage was so bad that most people avoided them.

The Jeep Cherokee started the Sport Utility era. Gas mileage no longer mattered; we were going to save the planet in other ways. Everybody had to have a Jeep. Once it became clear that almost anybody could buy a Jeep, the hot item was the Explorer. Before long, somebody had to up the ante, and Range Rovers were the car of choice among the cognisenti. There were a few Toyota Land Cruisers in there, too, usually replacing the Scouts. Then, once they came out with a Range Rover that only cost $30,000, the real status conscious had to move up again.

The Hummer era lasted only a couple of years, but for a while there, we had several Hummers in town. They are a very practical car for a location like Park City. They are about 14 feet wide, so they take up a whole street in Old Town, even when parked. They get almost 6 miles to the gallon. They burn diesel so they leave a streak of soot behind them making it impossible to get lost, and most importantly, they are terribly uncomfortable. I only rode in a Hummer once, and it was worse than riding on a hay swather in a field full of mole tunnel mounds. Loud, smelly, and rough. But what do you want for $80,000? I personally found the Hummer era to be quite disturbing. I'm not sure what it says about a community when people think they need a military assault vehicle to drive to the grocery store.

The Hummer owners have mostly gone underground. I suspect that the Hummers are still there, parked in spare garages and fitted with machine guns waiting for the revolution. But trying to find somebody who will admit to owning a Hummer is as hard as finding somebody who will admit to voting for Nixon. You still see a Hummer around town now and then, occupying four parking spaces (but feeding the meter only once). The driver is usually some second home owner, a guy with a bad comb-over, who doesn't spend quite enough time in town to keep up with local trends. The hot item now seems to be the Ford Expedition, which is almost as big as a Hummer, but a little more refined, and doesn't seem to carry the religious significance of a Suburban.

But before you can even take delivery on your new Dodge Dakota, the ever shifting trends have moved on. We are entering the Ferrari phase in Park City. They are beautiful cars. I got to ride in one once a couple of years ago. A friend who lives back east has one, and we drove it to the grocery store on twisty New England roads to pick up a few items. At mach 2. I didn't ask how it handled on snowy roads, or whether the mud on the unpaved road in to my house would be a problem in the spring, or how the annual insurance bill stacked up against my annual income. None of that matters. They are spectacular cars.

I'd buy one in a heartbeat, except that there's no place for the dog to ride.

Chapter 5

Some
Personal
Favorites

February 28, 1991

A TALE OF TWO MOUNTAINS

It was the best of times; it was the worst of times.
Well, maybe that stretches the point a little, since both were
really good times, they were just very different. Over the last
week, I got a chance to ski at Deer Valley one day and Alta the
next. It's a tough job, but somebody has to do it. I've skied at
both resorts in the past, but with a pass at Park City, it's easy to
end up at the same place all the time. The contrast between
Alta and Deer Valley is amazing.

The differences are pretty obvious right in the parking
lot. Deer Valley has pavement, and there are landscaped berms
between the lots so that even from the middle of a parking lot,
you don't see a shopping mall-style sea of parked cars. The
shuttle picks you up and delivers you to the base of the lift.

Alta finally paved most of their parking lots, but
probably because the Forest Service made them because of the
mud washing down the stream. There is no shuttle; you came
here for exercise, what's this with the shuttle business? From
the upper lots, there are stairways that look like something
from Dante's *Inferno* leading down to the base of the lifts, and
at the end of the day, there are rope tows (yeah, honest to
goodness rope tows on loan from the Smithsonian) to drag
your tired and battered body back up to the lodge. You still get

to climb the stairs under your own power, but it's only about four stories. Whiners will be thrown out in the snow.

Deer Valley is a fairly modest mountain with its trails groomed, graded, and "built" so that even a novice can ski like a World Cup Racer on about the second day out, or at least feel like one. Alta is an intimidating mountain, and absolutely nothing has been done to take off the rough edges. Even experts come off the mountain feeling like novices at Alta.

Neon and day-glo colors have virtually vanished from Deer Valley this year because the fashion gurus said it was "out." Nobody at Deer Valley ever appeared in a ski suit that was "out." The neon craze never found its way to Alta. They are pretty well stuck in the Army surplus wool pants and ragg sweater days. Duct tape is part of the dress code.

It would be hard to get lost at Deer Valley. There are trail signs everywhere in English and Japanese. If you did get lost, there are all those houses along the runs, and, if you could get past the Rotweilers, you could stop in and borrow the phone (if the batteries in your cellular were dead). Alta has a sign at the bottom of each lift that gives the name of the lift and its closing time. Home is down; what more do you want to know?

I suppose that in the lodge dining rooms, there is some pretty good food at Alta, but on the mountain, it's canned chili served in the ambience of wet wool and old ski boots. Clean socks are not part of the program. Deer Valley's mountain food service is, to say the least, civilized. If, by some odd chance, a French fry should fall toward the floor at a Deer Valley restaurant, it is intercepted in mid-air. I think they have the same technology as the Patriot missile, but it's not used much since the Deer Valley clientele seldom starts food fights. I didn't want to look at the floor at the restaurant at Alta. There are some things we are better off not knowing.

The lifts at Deer Valley seem to stop frequently while the operators help skiers load or unload. When people fall loading the chairs at Deer Valley, somebody is there to help them up, dust them off, and send them on their way. The day I skied Alta, the lift never stopped. You hear stories about people who fall loading the chair, and lift operators using shepherd's crooks to yank them out of the way while the crowd in the line presses forward. People who fall at the top of the lifts are sometimes never heard from again until spring.

"Alta is for skiers," is a slogan they have used for years. It is serious skiing. Alta is definitely not for shoppers, gourmet diners, condo purchasers, or fashion modelers. Coming from Park City, with our single industry (which isn't skiing, by the way) the absence of real estate sales offices was almost spooky. Nothing was for sale. Alta is mostly on Forest Service land, so there is literally nothing to sell. All that land and no real estate. No ski-in/ski-out condos with their own snow covered cloverleaves. No homesites with drop dead views, or open houses on the hill.

It's not just the real estate that is missing. I think it would be hard to buy a t-shirt in Alta. There are a couple of little ski shops in the lodges, but the retail economy there probably makes Moscow's look brisk. You can shop in Sandy; at Alta you just ski.

Serious skiing: that's Alta. Skiing doesn't get any better. If you want any other kind of recreation, or that complete vacation package, you have to move on. At Alta, the mountain is everything. It is hard to imagine a more challenging mountain to ski on, more spectacular scenery, or more Spartan surroundings. Deer Valley offers a different kind of ski experience, but also takes care of every other possible need or whim. I could spend a week at Deer Valley and never leave the dessert counter at the Snow Park Lodge. At Deer Valley, the mountain is part of the whole resort atmosphere, but it is almost incidental. The atmosphere at Alta is athletic; Deer Valley has more of the cruise ship feel. Both have a certain clubiness about them, with people returning year after year, but the membership lists don't overlap very much.

If only there were some way to put McHenry's Beach at the bottom of High Rustler.

February 25, 1993

THE BLIZZARD OF '93

It's the little things that affect life in the end. Simple decisions or whims can pack big consequences. Last weekend, I nearly gave my life for a ham sandwich, and a gristly one at that. I was skiing in Jupiter Bowl, and had a sudden hankering for a ham sandwich. The people I was with all wanted to take one more run, but I was ready for lunch, and started down. I was half way up the Thaynes Chair when the world turned about 90 degrees up on end. One second, the snow was coming straight down, and the next minute it was coming horizontally from the right. The chair was swinging then bouncing like it does with a sudden stop.

That stomach twist that happens when the chair moves up and down is even more surprising when the rest of the world has vanished from view in a total white-out. The Blizzard of '93 had hit. It was one for the record books.

The feint of heart headed for home. Based on a lifetime of skiing here, I knew (I *thought* I knew) that it couldn't last for more than a few minutes at that velocity. I answered the siren call of a ham sandwich and fries. Getting to the Snow Hut in a blizzard so hard that I couldn't clearly see the tips of my own skis was an adventure. There weren't many people on the hill, so there were no collisions (at least I think that was a tree I smacked into). Lunch and a chance to dry out, let the weather

135

break, and then finish the day on the slopes with new snow all to myself; it was such a simple plan.

This was no ordinary snow storm. The windows of the Snow Hut were bulging in and out by a full inch. The building itself kind of shuddered. As each new group came in, shaking snow out of their sleeves, pant legs, and pockets, it was obvious that nothing was letting up at all. It may have been getting worse. I decided to hit the road and call it a day. But the lift was closed. It took a while to figure that out because from the Snow Hut deck, I couldn't even see the lift.

Trapped, I went back inside to wait it out with the rest of the crowd. Beer sales took a sharp up-turn as the crowd tried to gain position. Shaquille O'Neal would have had a hard time holding a spot on the floor. Without referees, there were elbows being thrown here and there, and several very personal fouls were observed.

Anytime the power of nature is that apparent, there is a sense of fear, or at least anxiety. Our vulnerability becomes pretty apparent. The storm was not letting up, and visibility was so bad that skiing out seemed impossible. The group in the corner by me was expressing concern about avalanche. A local contractor was reminiscing about various structural problems with the building when it was over-loaded. Somebody else was afraid of missing the NBA Legends game at the Delta Center. Another couple was afraid they would have to try to re-arrange their flight schedule on Morris Air.

If that wasn't frightening enough, I was thinking about the prospect of spending the night in the Snow Hut with 500 of my closest friends who had been loading up on chili and beer for several of hours. If we didn't get out before it started getting dark, the mood would turn incredibly ugly.

It was still a raging storm. For the first time, I believed the story about a distant cousin on my Dad's side who disappeared in a blizzard on his way back from the outhouse. He was never found again, but they did locate the Sears catalog in the spring. Three little girls who had been sitting across from me at lunch had frostbite on their cheeks.

Resort manager Phil Jones showed up to try to calm the situation. He was matter of fact and reassuring. He inspired confidence and cooperation. Then something happened that was far more frightening than avalanche, asphyxiation, and the price of ski resort hot dogs combined. He said one word and almost started a stampede: "Refund." The crowd nearly rushed the table Phil was standing on like fans at a rock concert. I dried out my goggles (not that it mattered, there was nothing to see) and went back outside to wait in the storm where it was safer. Being trampled in a stampede of people who were going to get their money back on a ski pass because the weather turned rotten is a lot worse than vanishing in a blizzard.

A few minutes later, Phil Jones came outside. I couldn't help but notice that he was not wearing a hat. I've known Phil Jones since he was a rookie ski instructor. I've never seen him wearing a hat, no matter how bad the weather is. He says it's bad for business; gives people the fool notion that it's cold outside.

So everybody waited it out. The ski patrol did their stuff, preparing for the emergency evacuation down Thaynes Canyon to the golf course. I don't know how they could "sweep" the mountain under those conditions, but while the rest of us were in the relative comfort of the Snow Hut, the ski patrol was out there on the hill checking to make sure nobody was stuck head first in a drift. Several people were evacuated from chair lifts with ropes. They earn their passes several times a year, but Saturday, the ski patrol, instructors, and lift crew members who quickly organized to deal with the situation earned the respect of everybody on the mountain.

The wind died down to a mere gale, and they made the decision to take us all up the King Con lift, then down Gotcha Cut-off to the Resort Center. One member of the lift crew was standing on top of a tower, with the wind screaming around him, holding the automatic shut off switch so the lift would keep moving. That guy deserves a medal, and a trip to Barbados.

Anyway, if I had done the sensible thing when the world turned sideways, and found my way down to the parking lot, I would have missed a gristly ham sandwich and most of the Blizzard of '93. I owe it all to a ham sandwich.

And I couldn't help remember Mama Cass Elliott, the hefty singer with the Mamas and the Papas (which puts me safely beyond the snowboard generation). According to popular rumor if not fact, it was a ham sandwich that did her in. The story goes that she choked on a ham and swiss in a New York deli; died right on the spot. Things can always be worse.

But I think I might try tuna next time.

March 22, 1997

401(k) COFFEE

The other night I was sorting through a pile of papers trying to get my taxes figured out enough to pass it all off to an accountant. It used to be that my accountant was just starting out, and he appreciated getting a truckload of disorganized paper dumped on his desk because he needed the work. Not any more. Now he expects me to have brought some order to the process. Not much, but some.

In the process of going over the books, such as they are, I got looking at retirement stuff. The gap between what I earned and what was left over seemed pretty good at the end of the year, and there ought to have been something for retirement savings. But when it came to actually locating that cash, well, it was gone. I looked everywhere--under the couch cushions, in the washing machine, everywhere. I even looked in unlikely places like my checking account.

The obvious conclusion was that I had been the victim of some terrible embezzlement scheme. It's like Enid Waldholtz had been doing my bookkeeping, and it was just gone. Slowly, the sad tale began to unwind, and I discovered where it had gone. In the words of Joe Waldholtz, I spent it.

That is the lament of my generation. The options are to live modestly and save for retirement, or ski on really nice gear and have a fully suspended carbon fiber mountain bike, and spend the golden years eating Top Raman noodles. Ten years ago, the choice was obvious. As the Top Raman days begin to appear on the horizon, well, it's less clear.

I was moaning about this with my old friend Walt the dry wall hanger the other day. Walt has returned to his normal self after a binge of living large. He has finally realized that he can't do his job from a beach in Mexico. His cell phone bills were bigger than the house payment, and he wasn't getting any work done. He's sold the Range Rover for a top of the line Dodge truck, and is back at it. We were lunching on mass produced pizza instead of free-range chicken pesto.

Walt confessed that he hadn't been very good about saving for retirement, either, and that he was beginning to realize that there were limits to how many years he would be able to hang drywall before the minor aches and pains got to be serious. But Walt is not one to worry. He's always got a plan.

"I've got it figured out," he said. "I'm going to drive out there to McDonalds and get me a cup of that 401(k) coffee they serve."

I didn't understand.

"McDonalds serves hot drinks, coffee, tea, and probably hot chocolate that is so hot it will blister the paint on a Hummer. All you have to do is order a cup to go, spill a little on your leg, and sue the bejeezus out of them. Then the judgment funds your retirement account."

"Well, I don't think it is quite that automatic. It's not like the toy with the Happy Meal. I don't think you get to drive through the drive-up window, dump the coffee, and leave with a bag of cash."

"Of course not. Retirement takes planning. You have to have a good witness right there in the front seat with you. I always take a friend who is a pastry chef along with me when I go to Mickey D's, just in case. She carries her candy thermometer right in her purse. She can get an instant reading on the temperature of the coffee. It's also good to have a doctor there who can assess the severity of the burns, but you can always get that at the clinic. But the candy thermometer and a good witness are essential. I never leave home without them."

"But Walt, I don't think it counts if you spill hot coffee on your leg on purpose. Doesn't the spill have to happen because of something McDonald's did, like leaving the lid off the cup, or the employee dumping it on you? Doesn't their negligence play into this?"

"You'd think so, but the cases so far say that all they have to do is serve you coffee hotter than the industry standard, and you hold the cup in your bare hands for a second or two, then yell 'Yoweee!' and drop it right in your lap. Then wait for the checks to start rolling in."

While demonstrating this, Walt got a little carried away and held up a glass of Coke, yelled his "Yowee!" and dropped it, even though it was basically room temperature. It spilled all over the table, and the waitress was staring daggers at us. It was the kind of mess a two-year old would make. But spilling on the table doesn't cause burns. Walt will have to practice his aim. "You want to hit right here on the leg," he said. "Not too high, if you know what I mean."

I wasn't sure about any of this.

"Or, if you don't want to retire at McDonalds, you can take a slice of pizza and take a big bite out of it and burn the inside of your mouth." He demonstrated this with our now Coke soaked and cold pizza. He took a big bite, then dropped his jaw, rolled his eyes in mock pain, and keeled over backwards in his chair shouting for water and choking.

The waitress immediately produced our check, and stood there until we came up with the cash.

As we walked back to our cars, Walt gave me several other suggestions for funding a retirement program in a hurry. "The new floor in the Post Office is perfect. It's slick as glass right now. Just wait for it to get good and wet, and bingo, you just joined the Postal Service Pension Plan."

141

"But Walt, to really collect on any of these things, don't you have to be seriously injured--broken bones and permanent disabilities? They don't pay off big time just because you slipped or spilled your coffee."

"Well, there is that. But what kind of retirement fund can you really expect for the price of a lousy cup of McDonald's coffee? Nobody said saving for retirement would be easy."

June 22, 1996

FREE THE MOWERS

It's funny how you can mark certain life changes right down to the second. Some things sneak up on you gradually like bald spots or the need to add an inch to the waist size when you buy pants. But other things are immediate. I can recall the exact time and place when I became a Republican. It was pretty alarming.

I bought a new lawn mower. For all the years I've had my house in Woodland, I've used the mower that was next door at my mother's house. It was a big, solid, bullet proof mower that my Dad bought from Hoyt's general store in Kamas when I was about 10 years old. I remember the purchase pretty well because we had gone into the grocery store for a quart of milk and left with a lawn mower instead. The old mower is at least 30 years old, and was shared among several houses. It was starting to self destruct, and even the welds where we had welded the handles back together had welds.

So I bought a new mower. The political significance of a new lawn mower is not immediately clear. I pulled it out of the truck and poured oil and gas in it, then pulled the rope. That was the instant that I became a Republican. All it took was pulling the rope.

As a child of the suburbs, I've seen my share of lawn mowers. They are basic machines, not much advanced from the lever or pulley. A child of 10 can run a mower, and in most

143

households (exclusive of Park City where being seen mowing your own lawn is the kind of social gaffe that will start rumors of bankruptcy) that's what kids are for. So there really is no need to read the instructions on a lawn mower. Pull the rope and cut the grass.

No way. This is one of those new mowers with all the government required safety crap built into it. To start the mower, you have to stand with both feet on the front porch, and your left hand grasping three different levers. Carbon dioxide and motion sensors disable the engine if there is any other life form within a quarter mile. With your right hand, you can pull the rope. I don't think a left handed person could ever start this mower. The rope isn't down on the engine where it's supposed to be. It's rigged up through a bunch of guides so the end to yank the rope is up at the push handle on the mower. You can only start the mower while standing so far away from it that you can't reach it.

The elegance of this design is wonderful to see. Instead of being able to assume the traditional stance of the victorious hunter with one foot on top of the mower engine, holding it down while you give the rope a manly pull, you yank the rope and tip the mower over because the angle of the pull is about like a curtain rod instead. The old stance, with the foot on the mower and the position of man's dominance over both machine and the encroaching jungle dated back to the days when our hairy ancestors were killing lions with sharp sticks.

Starting the mower was one thing. Actually mowing the lawn was another. The new mower has this second bar under the push handle. You have to hold that up against the handle, and if you let go, even for a second, it stops the engine. So if you let go of the mower to bend down and move the hose, the engine dies. At first I thought this was a manufacturing defect, but was shocked to read in the manual that they actually designed this feature into the mower on purpose. The federal government has decided that lawn mowers are a matter of national security.

I don't want the federal government protecting me from the dangers of lawn mowers. I know lawn mowers are capable of cutting things--that is, after all, what we buy them for. Now you wouldn't think that a safety feature on the lawn mower would set me off that way, but it did. My dog fills the yard with sticks and other items she drags home. When you mow the yard only a couple of times a year, like I do, the grass gets pretty deep and you have to watch for this stuff carefully. So I was constantly letting go of the mower's magic handle and bending over to toss something out of the way. And the engine would stop.

The main reason I mow the yard at all is that the mosquitoes are so thick in the deep grass that they are carrying livestock away. Mowing a little patch around the house seems to discourage them in a more acceptable way that dousing everything with DDT or burning old tires. So while I'm pushing the mower around the yard, I'm also swatting at mosquitoes and slapping my legs, arms, and back. Every time I'd go for a mosquito, the mower would die because I'd taken my hand off the magic button.

Well, you don't spend as many years as I have on a farm without learning a thing or two about defeating the safety switches on machinery. I got out a roll of duct tape and taped the magic switches in the "run" position, which worked fine except that there is no way to turn the mower off when it's actually time to turn it off and put it back in the garage. The only "off" switch is the safety cut off that I had just disabled. Disabled is maybe not strong enough. In my frustration I had more or less wrapped the safety switch and the handle together like a duct tape mummy. It finally ran out of gas before I could cut all the tape off.

The old mower used to shut off by shorting out the spark plug, which was exposed on the side of the engine and frankly presented more risk of injury than the blade of the mower. I always pushed the little metal tab that shorted it out with my foot instead of my finger because the tab was bent and sometimes didn't make good contact and instead of turning off the mower, it electrocuted the operator. But it worked.

As I mowed the lawn, and wore out the starter rope re-starting after every mosquito attack, I got wondering why the Democrats would care so much if people lost a finger or two in lawn mower mishaps. After all, the odds are pretty good that the owner of the large suburban lawn is voting Republican anyway. A worker who lost a finger or toe to an unsafe mower might sue the pants of him. Newt Gingrich wouldn't care, because the guy he hires to mow his lawn probably voted Democrat, and if he lost a few fingers, he may not be able to work the voting machine. The guy Pat Buchanan hires to mow his lawn is an illegal immigrant. There is a certain Darwinian justice in allowing people who stick their hands under a running lawn mower to suffer the consequences.

So if you notice that my yard is even more over-grown and unkempt this year than usual, keep in mind that it's not sloth. It's an act of revolution. I'm not mowing the yard with any federally regulated mower.

May 4, 1996

ROOMING WITH MARTHA

So here it is, the first Saturday edition of the Park
Record. I'm not sure if this is the second paper of last week, or
the first issue of this week, but either way, the production staff
cranked out two papers inside of seven days and, with some
minor exceptions, made it through without injury. There were a
few threats of mayhem, and we did have to lock up the scissors
for a while, but otherwise it went smoothly.

This is a big deal for the paper. There has been a lot of
discussion about whether it is all for the better. I mean, do you
really want to read the details of the City Council meeting that
much sooner? Some things are probably better left alone, or at
least make better news after they have had a chance to breathe a
little. Two papers a week assumes that there will be news
happening in nice, even increments, and that people out there
will actually generate that much news.

I've always wanted to run a banner headline, one of
those "above the masthead" things normally reserved for
presidential assassinations, the outbreak of war or royal
divorces, that said "Nothing Happened!" There are weeks like
that around here, especially this time of year. Frankly, it would
be nice if there were more of them.

Instead, when there isn't news, we have to create it.
"Paper Cut Outbreak Plagues Middle School," "County Adopts
Noxious Weed Ordinance," "Planners Ponder Dog House
Design." I guess we could just re-print last week's news until

something fresh comes along. It works for other news organizations.

The move to twice a week has made some changes internally, too. There are some new features in the paper, and some new faces around the office. You can imagine my shock when I arrived at the office to find that I was now sharing my desk with Martha Stewart. Yeah, that's right, Martha will be doing a column for the paper now (the Wednesday paper had a great piece on Spring Cleaning that will have even the most compulsive feeling like a slacker), and since we are both part timers, management decided we could share a work space. Of course, I was not consulted about this in advance.

Sharing a desk with Martha Stewart is about my worst nightmare. I'm not a complete slob, but if they were doing a production of the "Odd Couple," there is no question I would be in the running for the Oscar Madison role. Martha makes Felix Unger look like a barbarian.

My first clue that something was up was when I walked in and noticed the desk. My stuff was still there, but it was different. For example, there has been a little pile of greasy bicycle parts sitting on the corner of the desk since last fall. I planned to take them with me when I bought the replacements to be sure I got all the right stuff. Well, they are still there, but instead of soaking into an old press release from Orrin Hatch's office, somebody had washed the spooge off, applied a little silver polish, attached a polished granite base, and put a doily under them. It looks like high-tech decorator art.

The row of Styrofoam coffee cups from Subway were gone. There was nothing special about them, and I wasn't going to drink the last little bit of week old, cold coffee in the bottom anyway, but they were gone. In their place was a plain, bone white ceramic mug. With a matching saucer. No logo on it at all. I didn't know you could get a coffee mug that didn't have advertising for somebody on the side of it, but there it was, a simple white mug. And next to it, a matching vase with fresh cut flowers.

I keep track of things to do and ideas that are rattling around loose in my head by writing them down on yellow post-it notes and sticking them on the wall above the desk. That way, aside from the fact that I can't read my own handwriting, and the multiple layers of post-it notes with the more important ones buried in the Pleistocene era under piles of more recent notes, I have everything within reach for easy retrieval.

Well, imagine my surprise to find that somebody had scraped them all off the wall and replaced them with a nice print of some bucolic French country scene. And my post-it note index to life had been reduced to a leather bound three ring binder with each one neatly typed, categorized, and cross indexed to other post-it notes on related topics.

There was a very nice pen and pencil set on the desk. It looked highly professional and somehow the importance of all future notes will seem greater because they have been written with such dignified writing instruments, instead of your basic yellow pencil with tooth marks on it. A reminder to "pick up pizza" on the way home will never be the same. I might not even be able to eat pizza if the reminder note has to be done in calligraphy on real parchment.

When I mentioned that to Martha, she just gave me that sinister little smile of hers, and said that I probably could adjust to a life where dinner was more special than re-heated pizza eaten standing over the kitchen sink. Like I'm going to dirty a plate or something.

It was just different, having Martha Stewart hanging around. I don't feel like I can put my feet on the desk anymore because it will get the linen table cloth dirty. The bag of Hershey Kisses that is about half Kisses and half the balled-up wrappers from the ones I already ate has been replaced with a little silver bowl. I don't know where to put the wrappers, but shooting them across the aisle at Nan or Brian doesn't seem appropriate any more. There isn't even any chocolate on the keyboard.

It's not all bad, having to share a desk with Martha. Instead of Circle K doughnuts out of a paper bag, we now snack on home baked French pastries served from little baskets in the morning. Everybody gets a plate, and the pastries are served with tongs. There are cloth napkins instead of paper towels or back issues of the paper to wipe our hands on. It all feels very luxurious.

But there is something insidious about Martha's obsessive compulsive behavior. Once she starts working on a place, there is just no stopping her. It starts with the post-it notes stuck to the wall, then yesterday's half eaten jelly doughnuts are gone, and sooner or later, I'm afraid she will be cleaning the ski wax off the bottom of the iron and teaching the whole staff how to press a shirt.

No wonder Luke Smith packed it in to move to Montana.

April 2, 1992

TRIBAL HUNTER-GATHERERS STRIKE

We've all had this experience: You are trying to pick up a few grocery items at Albertson's after work, not a major shopping spree, but just the couple of things you are out of and need to fix that night's dinner. You charge in the store, and find grid lock. People in expensive ski suits are standing four and five abreast in the aisles, discussing the relative merits of one brand of cooking oil over another. It looks like a high fashion sit-in.

Southern voices say they don't know these brands-- things are different at the Winn Dixie or Kroger store at home. There isn't any okra in the whole store, canned or fresh, and nobody has heard of grits ("You might try on the hardware aisle.")   There are a half dozen people gathered around the milk cooler trying to decide between a gallon and a half gallon, 2% or skim. After watching this for about ten minutes, you realize that this crowd is not made up of six separate hunter-gatherers each buying milk. The six of them are a single tribe, and together they buy a quart--one quart--for their coffee in the morning, then move on to discover that the egg shells in this part of the country are white, not brown.

You know the pattern, grocery shopping by committee. It is often a committee made up of people who are not used to grocery shopping. Husbands who have generously let their

151

wives stay back at the condo to rest up after skiing are turned loose in a strange store without benefit of a shopping list. "I can't remember which cartoon character's cereal my kids eat. Do you think it's this Quaker guy?" These folks are truly out of their element, looking at brands they may never have heard of. "Who's this Janet Lee, anyway?" "We always buy the stuff in the red can at home, but they don't have it here."

As you push your cart up and down the hardware aisle to avoid the crowd, you can't help but wonder how it can be so hard to pick up a few things to eat. We all have our strategies worked out, and know where to park the cart and which aisles you can make good time on and which to avoid. I've found the beer/potato chip and breakfast cereal aisles are the most congested. Pet supplies is like a freeway; a regular "locals only" express lane to the eggs and lunch meat.

I used to be the worst for complaining about the tribal hunting party approach to shopping, but I have been reformed. I understand it now. On a recent weekend trip with a group of friends, I was part of the designated hunter-gatherer committee sent to the market. It was a classic get out of town and make plans later kind of trip, so grocery shopping was not part of the preparations. With five hours in the car, there was no time to discuss what to eat. We just pulled up at the market.

We started out with the grocery procurement committee pushing a cart up and down the aisles, stopping to discuss each item. Whole wheat or white rolls, turkey or red meat for the sandwiches (Ham is kind of pink, and required extra explanation.) How much spaghetti sauce do we need, which brand? I think it was at the spaghetti sauce that we all suddenly realized that we had become the very people we had been dealing with all winter, and had gone on vacation to get away from. Locals were trying to get around us, giving that same "Welcome to our town, but speed up your shopping, ok?" smile we have all seen in the mirror.

It was like a bomb went off. We scattered into the four corners of the store, each grabbing what looked good and what we thought would improve dinner. We made eye contact up and down the aisles, and parked the cart in a central place. After twenty minutes at the bottled spaghetti sauce, we managed to complete the shopping trip in about five minutes. Those skills we have been practicing at Albertson's all season were in perfect form. Confused tourists actually flagged me down to ask about items they couldn't find. It was the perfect grocery store blitz.

But there is something else about this committee shopping spree. People eat differently. In fact, some perfectly normal people eat things I've never heard of before. I was afraid that the whole process was falling apart when I got back to our cart and found foodstuffs from Mars mixed in with "my" groceries. Right there next to the Double Stuff Oreos was a package of rice cakes, those things that look like foam building insulation cut-outs. The Sugar Frosted Flakes were being paired up with some kind of granola so natural it is sold in a burlap bag instead of a box with cartoon characters on it. It weighs about six pounds per serving. Mineral water right there with a six pack of Coke.

I said to myself, as I pushed this mixed bag to the check stand, this is going to be some interesting eating. No wonder those people in Albertson's are not willing to split up the job. We were shopping for a couple of meals. Almost anything's tolerable for that long. But if you were shopping for a week-- an expensive week--there is no way you would trust even your closest friend to buy the right breakfast cereal. If you're a Folgers man, waking up to find MJB on the table is not the stuff of dream vacations. What if your traveling companion buys de-caf? Or that chemical creamer? Or rice cakes for heaven's sake. Rice cakes.

For years, I have been under the impression that grocery clerks never notice what you buy. It is a matter of

153

professionalism. If they secretly think "What in the world is this guy going to do with two quarts of transmission fluid and a cake decorating kit?" the typical grocery checker doesn't even raise an eyebrow. But there was a definite curl on the lip of the checker when she pulled the Twinkies and alfalfa sprouts out of the cart in the same handful. We were all standing there in the checkstand, and the clerk looked us over pretty carefully.

It all worked out. We ate well and snacked well, and before the weekend was out, everybody attained a common dietary level, with Double Stuff Oreo crumbs on every face. The rice cakes seem to have made it back to Park City unopened, but we did polish off the carrots and the broccoli. And it's a good thing that there is that kind of variety available in the grocery stores. Life would be kind of limited if the only things available were Double Stuff Oreos and pecan sweet rolls. Not bad, just limited.

And I will confess that there is even a place in the world for rice cakes, particularly during Lent, assuming of course that you happen to be Catholic and have a lot of mortal sin on your hands.

November 30, 1996

HAPPY THANKSGIVING

My sister tells a story about one of her friends and their Thanksgiving celebration. I'm not sure I've got all the details right, and maybe for purposes of libel insurance, it's best that some liberties are taken to conceal the identities of the parties. The story is about a typical Thanksgiving celebration at my sister's friend's house. I've met the couple, and while they don't live in Park City, they would fit right in. Their house is huge, located in the right neighborhood, and decorated in a style that makes attractive magazine photos but would be hard to actually live in because everything was so perfectly arranged.

The couple has five or six children, each the paragon of age-appropriate behavior ranging from a kid in elementary school to a newly-wed just completing college. The children are all attractive and fit with the decor of the house nicely. They have been brought up well, and know which fork to use and how to behave at a nice dinner.

The couple owns a successful business that, in the years leading up to the story, had seen phenomenal growth and added a number of employees. It was featured in a national magazine about businesses that were good places to work, where the owners and managers really cared about the well being of the work force. Times were exceptionally good.

When the Thanksgiving Feast was put on the table, it was served up on silver platters and antique China. Each piece had a pedigree, some going back to the wife's family arriving in

Plymouth on the Mayflower. The scene was Normal Rockwell with computer enhancements and Martha Stewart flourishes. After a lengthy blessing on the food, as the serving plates started moving around the table heaped with more food than they could eat in a week, the hostess said that she wanted each of them to go around the table and, in the midst of all this bounty, say what they were thankful for. They would start at the head of the table with the husband.

He paused for a moment, and then announced that he was "Thankful we don't live in Bosnia."

The hostess burst into tears. Great-Grandmother's silver tarnished on the spot. The children broke out with acne.

Now I've found that this story has some gender-based comprehension problems. Women, as a general rule, understand why the response "I'm thankful we don't live in Bosnia," was so poorly received. It has something to do with a week of preparation for the meal and getting up at 4 a.m. to put a 25 pound turkey in the oven, and nobody commenting on the center piece, etc. etc. My sister had to explain all of that to me.

Men, on the other hand, hear the line, "I'm thankful we don't live in Bosnia," and find something entirely different. They see a remarkable economy of language that covers, in a few words, the incredible breadth of all we have to be grateful for. There is a simple eloquence there that the poor guy had probably been practicing for several days leading up to the celebration. Life in Bosnia (still, but at the time even more so) defines the antithesis of everything we have here. If life in a safe, clean suburb surrounded by healthy, happy family members basking in economic security is one extreme, Bosnia is the complete opposite. Saying you are thankful you don't live in Bosnia may not be the most direct way of saying you love and appreciate your wife and family and home and country, but nine out of ten guys interviewed agreed that it got the job done.

But apparently they were wrong.

*   *   *

I took a spontaneous day off work and skied on the new "six-pack lift" the second day it was open. The permutations of passenger combinations are remarkable. A couple of times I was on it alone, feeling like the only person at the matinee in a big theater. Once I was on with a full six-pack load of telemark skiers. Another was a mixed batch of snow boards, antique skis used three times a year on vacation, and the hottest new parabolic shaped skis. The only element missing was a para-Olympian in one of those sit-ski things. It's pretty fun, and really moves up the hill. They still need to work out the top a little, though. The chair stops so suddenly it leaves skid marks. A lawyer from Los Angeles was passing out whiplash collars with his phone number printed on them. It's great to get out and enjoy skiing this early, to feel the muscles stretch a little and breath in the fresh air on the mountain.

The propane delivery guy finally decided the road into my house had frozen solidly enough he dared drive on it, and got the tank filled up. There's something nice about knowing that there is a big stack of wood for the stove, and a full tank of propane for the furnace sitting there in the yard. The house will be warm and dry this winter. The dog wanders from a sunny spot in the dining room to the warm spot in front of the wood stove. She sleeps on her back, with her feet in the air and her belly exposed. The biggest risk in her life is that I might get distracted and walk past without pausing to rub her belly.

I spent Thanksgiving in Salt Lake at my mother's house. We've generally celebrated out at the ranch in Woodland, but it didn't work out this year for a lot reasons. Mom has lived in the house in Salt Lake for nearly 50 years, and not a lot has changed since we were kids growing up there. I still know where even the more obscure, Thanksgiving-and-Christmas-only pots and pans are kept. I half expect to find Dad sitting in the den napping through the football games, even though it's been five years since he died. Things just feel like home around there.

Over the weekend, the whole family, with nieces and nephews and grand-nieces and nephews came out to Woodland for the annual Thanksgiving Weekend broom hockey game on the pond behind the house. We ate too much pie and told the same stories we tell every year.

Boy, am I glad I don't live in Bosnia.